Ernest Shackleton

ERNEST SHACKLETON

GRIPPED BY THE ANTARCTIC

Rebecca L. Johnson

Carolrhoda Books, Inc./Minneapolis

For Susan Rose, editor and friend

Carolrhoda Books, Inc.,
A division of Lerner Publishing Group
241 First Avenue North
Minneapolis, MN 55401 U.S.A.

Website address: www.lernerbooks.com

Library of Congress Cataloging-in-Publication Data

Johnson, Rebecca L.
Ernest Shackleton / by Rebecca L. Johnson.
p. cm. – (Trailblazer biography)
Includes bibliographical references.
Summary: A biography of Sir Ernest Shackleton, the daring, charismatic Antarctic explorer who fell short of his goal of crossing Antarctica but accomplished a far greater feat by bringing every member of his crew back alive.
ISBN: 0–87614–920–4 (lib. bdg. : alk. paper)
1. Shackleton, Ernest Henry, Sir, 1874–1922—Juvenile literature.
2. Explorers—Great Britain—Biography—Juvenile literature.
3. Antarctica—Discovery and exploration—Juvenile literature.
[1. Shackleton, Ernest Henry, Sir, 1874–1922. 2. Explorers.
3. Antarctica—Discovery and exploration.] I. Title. II. Series.
G875.S5 J65 2003
919.8'904—dc21 2002006816

Manufactured in the United States of America
1 2 3 4 5 6 – JR – 08 07 06 05 04 03

Contents

Ernest Shackleton's ship, *Endurance*, lies trapped in the sea ice off the Antarctic coast in January 1915.

Thrilling adventure stories sparked Ernest's imagination. More than anything, he wanted to find fame and fortune in far-off parts of the world.

1

An Adventuresome Lad

Ernest Shackleton stood on the deck of *Endurance.* A bitter Antarctic wind moaned through the ship's frozen rigging. Ernest—a short, ruggedly built Irishman—squinted beneath heavy brows against the glare. The view was the same in every direction. They were surrounded by jagged, glittering ice that stretched to the horizon under a pale polar sky.

It was January 15, 1915. For the past few weeks, *Endurance* had been sailing slowly through the pack—the floating jumble of icebergs and chunks of sea ice surrounding Antarctica. Just one day's sail from where Ernest had planned to land on the continent, the ship was frozen into the pack of sea ice. Ernest and the twenty-seven men under his command were stranded in one of the most inhospitable and dangerous places on the earth.

Ernest knew they could expect no rescue. No one in the world knew exactly where they were.

Ernest Shackleton was no stranger to Antarctica. He had wrestled with this continent before. And he had a remarkable talent for surviving when survival seemed impossible. He was determined to get his men back to civilization alive. Brave, daring, resourceful, and eternally optimistic, Ernest Shackleton was one of the greatest Antarctic explorers of all time.

Ernest Shackleton was born half a world away from Antarctica, in Ireland. His father, Henry Shackleton, owned a farm about thirty miles south of Dublin, Ireland's capital city. In 1872 Henry married Henrietta Letitia Sophia Gavan. Spirited, cheerful, and practical, Henrietta was known for her optimistic outlook on life. The young couple lived in a large stone house that overlooked the farm's gently rolling hills.

Henry and Henrietta's first child was a girl named Alice. Ernest Henry Shackleton came next, born on February 15, 1874. From an early age, Ernest was a bright, good-natured little boy, confident that he could tackle any challenge. His parents weren't surprised, for example, when Ernest announced he was going to tunnel through the earth to Australia—and then went out in the yard and started digging.

More girls were born to Henry and Henrietta in the next few years—Amy, Clara, and Eleanor. Ernest's sisters loved being with their brother, although he liked to tease and play tricks on them and other members of the household. Once he hid some of his mother's jewelry in the garden. Then he talked a maid into helping him dig for buried treasure. The maid was very excited when she and Ernest "discovered" the jewels. But she was a bit irritated later when she realized she'd been fooled.

Ernest's parents were usually forgiving of such behavior. Even when he got into trouble, more often than not Ernest flashed his irresistible smile and talked his way out of punishment.

Life on the farm was pleasant for Ernest. He was schooled at home by a governess. When Ernest wasn't working at his lessons, there were pastures to wander in, trees to climb, and animals to care for and keep as pets. But from his father's point of view, life on the farm was not so rosy. Crops were poor and land prices had fallen drastically. Henry needed to find a new way to support his growing family.

In 1880, when Ernest was six years old, the Shackletons moved to Dublin where Henry Shackleton studied to become a doctor. By 1884 he had completed his medical training. Henrietta packed up all their belongings, and the Shackletons left Ireland for England. They settled in a suburb of London called Sydenham. A stately brick house—Aberdeen House—became their new home. It was an exciting move for Ernest. Suddenly the ten-year-old Irish lad exchanged the quiet countryside for the bustling city of London, the heart of the British Empire.

As Ernest neared his twelfth birthday, his parents enrolled him in a private school. Fir Lodge Preparatory School was just down the lane from Aberdeen House. Ernest got along well there, although his Irish accent set him apart from his English classmates. If anyone made fun of how he rolled his r's or drew out his vowels, he was quick to defend himself—sometimes with his fists.

Most of the time, though, Ernest was easygoing and friendly. He was also turning into a handsome young man, with thick dark hair and large gray-blue eyes. Like his mother, Ernest always had a positive, optimistic outlook on life—at least that's the impression he gave other people. If Ernest was sad or worried about something, he rarely told anyone or let it show on his face. He was also good at capturing the attention of other people. Not all the boys at Fir Lodge liked Ernest. But they found him interesting because he was clever and often unpredictable.

In 1887, at the age of thirteen, Ernest left Fir Lodge to attend Dulwich College, a private school for older boys. Dulwich, too, was within walking distance of Aberdeen House. Dulwich College was a good school, but Ernest was not a particularly good student. He was a smart young man, but he was bored by his classes. Again and again, his report cards had the same message scrawled on them: "Could Do Better."

Part of the problem was that Ernest's father wanted him to become a doctor. The classes Ernest took at Dulwich were supposed to prepare him for that career. But he didn't want to be a doctor. He wanted to lead a much

Ernest Shackleton as a teenager at Dulwich College

more adventurous life, like the people he read about in books and magazines.

Books took Ernest to faraway places where people led lives that seemed much more interesting than his life at Dulwich. Many of the books that Ernest read were about the sea and sailors. He also loved books of poetry. He memorized poems by John Keats, William Wordsworth, Robert Browning, and Alfred, Lord Tennyson. And he often quoted lines of poetry to his friends and family members.

Every Saturday, Ernest curled up with the latest edition of *The Boy's Own Paper*. This weekly magazine was full of thrilling adventure stories that sparked Ernest's imagination. More than anything, he wanted to find fame and fortune in far-off parts of the world.

Caught up in daydreams, Ernest was often late to school. Breathless, he would rush into the classroom. But before his teacher could protest, Ernest would launch into a long, complicated, and fantastic explanation for why he was late. No one was really fooled—the stories obviously weren't true. But the way Ernest told them was so entertaining that even his teachers couldn't resist listening to them. Ernest's quick wit and clever tales saved him from detention many times.

At home, Ernest loved to entertain—and tease—his sisters and younger brother, Frank. The sisters numbered eight in all. In addition to Alice, Amy, Clara, and Eleanor, there were Kathleen, Ethel, Gladys, and Helen. As exasperating as Ernest could be, his sisters adored him.

As Ernest's second year at Dulwich passed, he grew more stubborn about becoming a doctor. Henry Shackleton was disappointed in his son's attitude. But he realized it was pointless to force Ernest into a career he didn't want. So when Ernest was fifteen, Dr. Shackleton agreed to let his son become a sailor on one condition: he had to finish school.

For Ernest, pursuing a career as an officer in the British Royal Navy was out of the question—only young men from wealthy families could afford it. Next best was the merchant navy, which trained young men to serve as

Ernest stands behind his brothers and sisters. His younger brother, Frank, is seated on the blanket. His sisters are, from left to right, Kathleen, Ethel, Clara, Amy, Eleanor, Alice, Gladys, and Helen.

sailors and officers on commercial ships of all kinds. With the help of his father and a distant cousin who had connections to the merchant navy, Ernest secured a place aboard a sailing ship. It was *Hoghton Tower,* owned by the North Western Shipping Company of Liverpool, England.

With a clear goal in sight, Ernest began to work hard at his studies. In the spring of 1890, having just turned sixteen, he surprised his teachers and family by finishing at Dulwich with grades that put him near the top of his class. With the last exam behind him, Ernest packed his bags and eagerly set off for Liverpool to join the crew of *Hoghton Tower.* They were bound for Valparaiso, Chile—halfway around the world.

Life at sea was hard work, spiced with real danger. To climb the masts in bad weather, with the ship pitching and rolling, took steady hands and nerves of steel.

2

Life at Sea

Hoghton Tower was a three-masted, square-rigged clipper ship. Clipper ships were the fastest sailing ships on the ocean. Ernest quickly discovered that they were a challenge to sail.

One of Ernest's first jobs aboard *Hoghton Tower* was to learn the ropes. More than two hundred ropes controlled the hundreds of yards of canvas sails and other parts of the ship's rigging. Each rope had a name. There were halyards and clew lines, braces and backstays. Each rope had to be tightened or loosened or tied in just the right way, at just the right time, to keep the ship on course.

Life at sea was hard work, spiced with real danger. To climb the masts in bad weather, with the ship pitching and rolling, took steady hands and nerves of steel. Ernest liked this new life. Every day was different, full of fresh challenges and adventures.

To get to Chile, *Hoghton Tower* sailed to the southern tip of South America, around a spit of land known as Cape Horn. The Horn was everything Ernest's shipmates told him it would be. High winds churned the frigid waters into towering waves that slammed into the ship and surged over its decks. When a wave hit particularly hard, *Hoghton Tower* would tip far over to one side for a few seconds. At first Ernest thought the ship would founder and sink.

A ship, similar to those Ernest learned to sail, rounds Cape Horn. For sailors, the stormy, frigid seas of Cape Horn were among the world's most challenging.

But every time this happened, the ship righted and sailed on. Ernest learned how much stress a ship could take in rough waters. He watched how the seasoned sailors steered and handled the sails. He also noticed how the captain gave orders, made decisions, and treated his crew with a firm but fair hand.

One storm followed close on the heels of the next. Days of battling wind and waves turned into weeks as *Hoghton Tower* crept slowly toward the Pacific Ocean. All the while, Ernest and the other members of the crew kept a sharp eye out for icebergs. The huge chunks of floating ice came from Antarctica, where they broke off the edges of the vast ice sheets that covered the continent. Somewhere in the interior of that wild and mysterious frontier lay the South Pole, the very bottom of the world.

After two months, *Hoghton Tower* sailed into the calmer waters of the Pacific Ocean. Ernest had survived "rounding the Horn." He and his shipmates were exhausted and relieved. The ship sailed up the western coast of Chile, past Valparaiso, to a small port town. For several weeks, the crew ferried cargo from the docks to the ship in small boats. Ernest learned how to handle the boats in the heavy surf that pounded the shore. When the ship's cargo hold was full, the captain set a course for the long journey back to England. *Hoghton Tower* docked in Liverpool in April 1891. In a single year, Ernest had traveled halfway around the world and back.

Seventeen-year-old Ernest decided that despite its hardships, a life at sea was what he wanted. He liked being on the move. Ernest chose to sign on again with *Hoghton Tower* with the goal of becoming an officer.

Over the next four years, Ernest sailed back and forth between England, South America, and the Far East. He rounded Cape Horn five more times. Life at sea transformed him from a boy into a strong, decisive young man who knew the sea and ships well. He got to know his shipmates well, too. On English ships, it was customary that officers—and young men like Ernest who were training to become officers—didn't associate with seamen, engineers, and other members of the crew. Officers were better educated and had a higher place in society. Making friends with someone from a lower class was frowned upon. But Ernest crossed that barrier. He socialized with officers and sailors alike. Aboard *Hoghton Tower,* Ernest earned the nickname Old Shacks along with a reputation for being out of the ordinary.

When Ernest wasn't working on deck, he often retreated to his tiny cabin to read. He consumed books on history, geography, and poetry. He also studied for his officer exams. In the summer of 1894, twenty-year-old Ernest passed his exams and earned the rank of second mate—the third in command after the captain and first mate. He left *Hoghton Tower* and signed on as second mate on *Monmouthshire,* a steamship owned by the Welsh Shire Line that shuttled cargo between China, Japan, and the Americas.

Steamships were replacing sailing ships all over the world. Powered by coal-fired engines, steamships didn't depend on the wind to travel. By going to work for the

Welsh Shire Line, Ernest was making sure his career was on the right path. Steam was the way of the future, and Ernest wasn't about to be left behind. In 1896 he easily passed his exams and was promoted to the rank of first mate.

In the summer of 1897, Ernest met Emily Dorman, a friend of his sister Kathleen. Emily was six years older than Ernest. She was tall and dark-haired and had a quiet strength that Ernest admired. They shared a love of books and poetry, especially the poems of Robert Browning. Each time Ernest saw Emily, he was more enchanted by her. It wasn't long before Ernest and Emily wanted to marry. Emily's father, who was a successful attorney in London, liked Ernest. He wasn't convinced, however, that Ernest Shackleton was a good candidate for a son-in-law because Ernest's salary at the Welsh Shire Line was too small to support a wife and family.

Ernest continued to travel the world. He was gone for months at a time. But wherever his job took him, Emily was never far from his thoughts. When Ernest was aboard ship, he wrote long letters to her in his cabin. He wrote about the sailors and officers he worked with and about what he was reading. More than anything else, Ernest's letters were full of frustration about not being able to marry Emily and his hopes that somehow the situation would change in the future. Since money seemed to be the biggest obstacle to married life, Ernest began to dream and scheme about ways to make more of it.

In 1898 Ernest passed another set of exams, and he was promoted to the rank of master. This meant he was qualified to command any kind of British ship anywhere in the world. Yet Ernest was restless and discontented. He couldn't see himself spending the rest of his life aboard ships that transported cargo around the world, even if he was in command. His career was respectable but not glamorous. And he certainly would never get rich doing it. Ernest saw his life as ordinary. He longed for a chance to do something extraordinary. He confided to a shipmate, "I think I can do something better. In fact, really, I would like to make a name for myself."

To impress Emily—and her father—Ernest left the Welsh Shire Line for a better-paying job with the Union Castle Line. Ships of the Union Castle Line transported mail between Britain and South Africa. Next to being in the Royal Navy, working for the Union Castle Line was the most prestigious job Ernest could hope for as a young officer. It also meant that he could spend more time in England and with Emily. But Emily's father still would not give his permission for Ernest and Emily to marry.

In the spring of 1900, on a trip to Africa, Ernest met a young soldier named Cedric Longstaff. Cedric was headed to South Africa, where Britain was fighting a war. In a conversation, Cedric mentioned his father—Llewellyn Longstaff. Ernest recognized the name immediately. Llewellyn Longstaff was a wealthy British industrialist. He was also a major supporter of the National Antarctic Expedition. Ernest knew about this expedition. It was going to be the first British exploration of Antarctica in sixty years.

Back in 1841, Sir James Clark Ross had been sent to explore Antarctica by the British Royal Navy. Ross's ships had been the first to sail through the vast expanse of sea ice—the pack—that surrounds the continent. They had reached 78° (78 degrees) south latitude. (Sailors used latitude to find their exact location on the earth—how far they were north or south of the equator. Mapmakers put 90° south at the South Pole, 90° north at the North Pole, and 0° at the equator.)

In 1898, the same year Ernest earned the rank of master, a Belgian explorer named Adrien de Gerlache had headed to Antarctica. His ship had been trapped in the pack of sea ice for almost a year before breaking free. In 1899 another explorer, Carsten Borchgrevink, had led a small group of men who had become the first people to spend the winter on the Antarctic continent. Borchgrevink's party had traveled across the frozen land to 78°58' south—60 minutes (60') equalling one degree of latitude. In breaking Ross's old record, Borchgrevink had sparked a race for the South Pole.

Ernest knew that many powerful people in Great Britain wanted a British explorer to be the first to reach the Pole. One of these was Sir Clements Markham, the president of the British Royal Geographical Society. Markham had convinced Llewellyn Longstaff to finance the National Antarctic Expedition. He had insisted that Robert Falcon Scott, a commander in the British Royal Navy, lead it.

Scott had never led an expedition of any sort. He had spent no time in polar regions. But the backers of the National Antarctic Expedition considered Scott's

Robert Falcon Scott, the Royal Navy commander who was chosen to lead the National Antarctic Expedition

inexperience a plus. The British admired people who attempted great things without training, confident that they could simply figure things out along the way.

From Ernest's point of view, the fact that Scott had no polar training meant that his own lack of experience would not disqualify him from the expedition. The frozen land at the bottom of the world might be just the place where Ernest Shackleton could make his fortune. He might even become famous in the process.

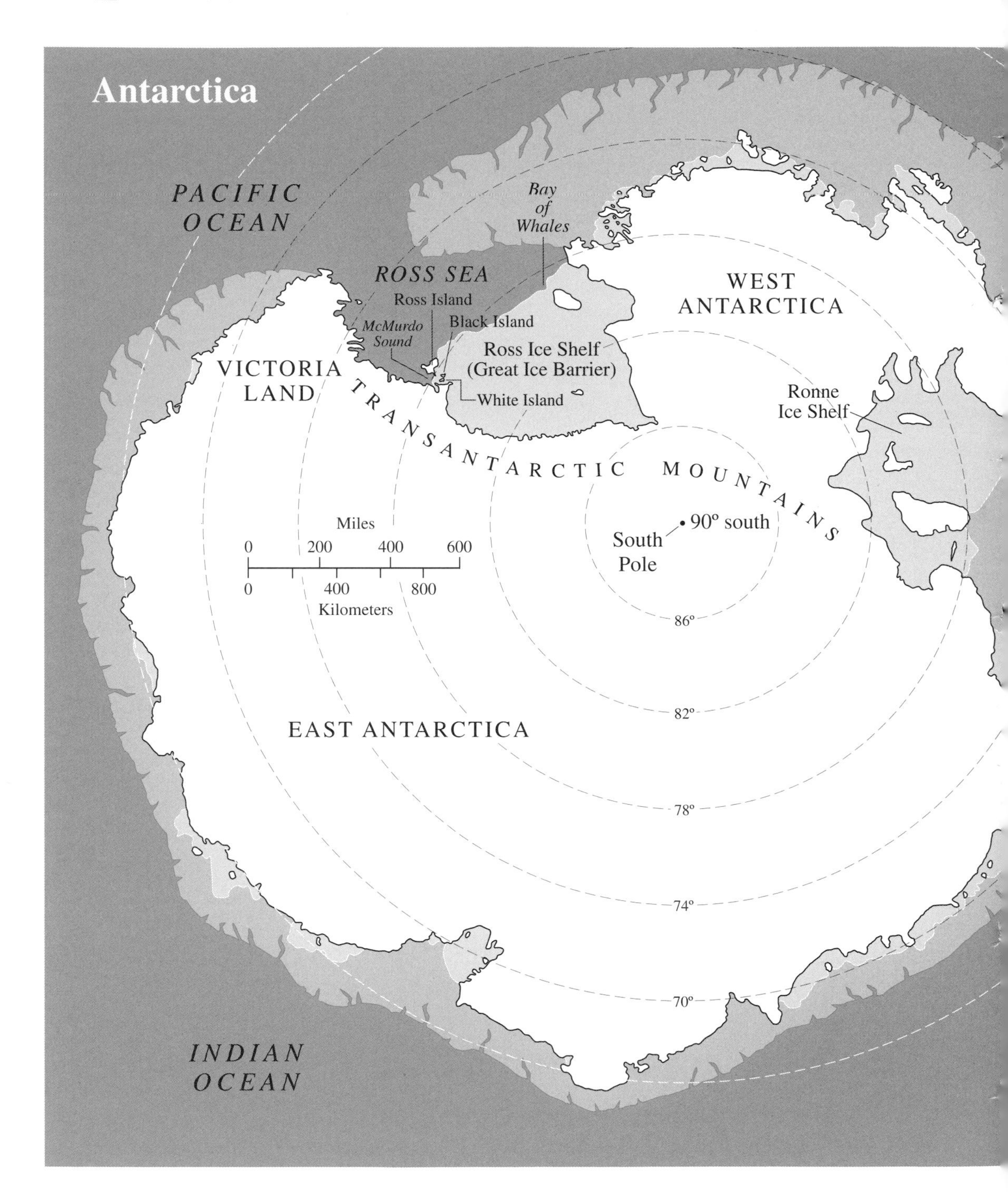
Antarctica
PACIFIC OCEAN
Bay of Whales
ROSS SEA
Ross Island
McMurdo Sound
Black Island
WEST ANTARCTICA
Ross Ice Shelf (Great Ice Barrier)
VICTORIA LAND
White Island
Ronne Ice Shelf
TRANSANTARCTIC MOUNTAINS
90° south
South Pole
Miles
0 200 400 600
0 400 800
Kilometers
86°
82°
EAST ANTARCTICA
78°
74°
70°
INDIAN OCEAN

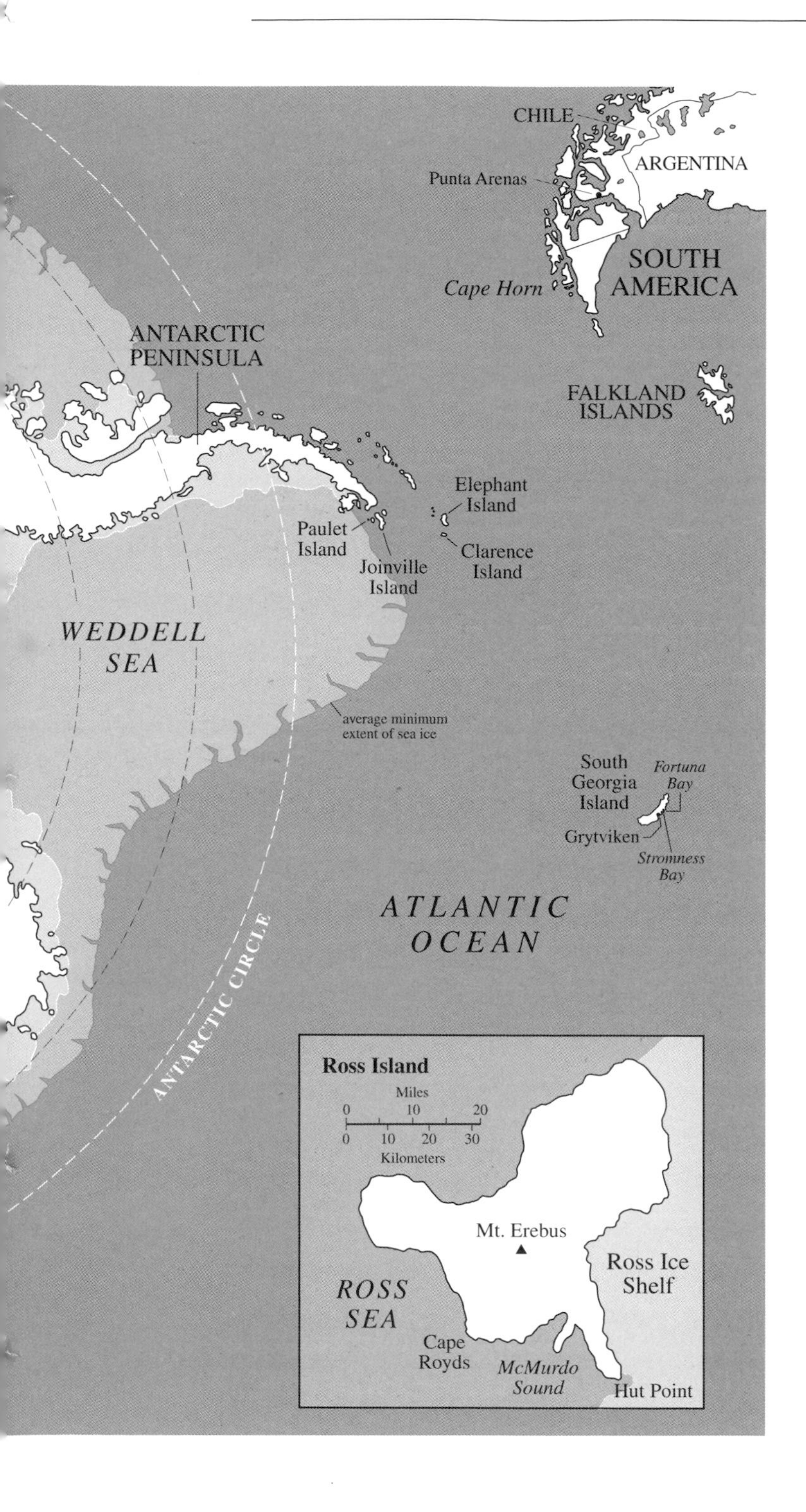

Explorers trying to reach the South Pole could go about it from two directions. They could sail from New Zealand to the Ross Sea and then set out across the Ross Ice Shelf (Great Ice Barrier). Or they could sail from South America, around the Antarctic Peninsula, to the Weddell Sea and then make their way across the Ronne Ice Shelf.

Ernest asked Cedric to write to his father. When Ernest returned to England, he met Llewellyn Longstaff. Ernest's enthusiasm and intensity impressed Longstaff. So when Ernest asked for help in joining the expedition to Antarctica, Longstaff agreed.

Ernest sailed for South Africa again. When he returned to England in March 1901, good news was waiting. Longstaff had recommended him to Markham. Ernest Shackleton had been accepted as a member of the National Antarctic Expedition.

If this was the way to the Pole, Shackleton thought, it didn't look terribly difficult. There were no mountains to climb, as far as they could see.

3

SOUTH WITH SCOTT

Ernest Shackleton and Robert Falcon Scott met at the National Antarctic Expedition offices in London. The two men were very different. Scott was tall and looked like an aristocrat. He was also reserved and a little condescending. Shackleton, broad-shouldered and compact, was his typical direct, intense, and enthusiastic self.

The two men were polite as they discussed the upcoming expedition. But there was a hint of tension, too. Scott was a member of the Royal Navy, while Shackleton came from the less socially prestigious merchant navy. Sir Clements had wanted all the officers in the National Antarctic Expedition to be "Royal Navy men." Shackleton realized he was looked upon as a sort of intruder into a special club. But that wasn't going to stop him.

Scott put Shackleton in charge of getting the expedition ship, *Discovery,* ready for the journey. Shackleton set to work immediately. There was no time to waste—the expedition was scheduled to set sail for Antarctica in less than six months. *Discovery* had been especially built for the expedition. It was a large, strong wooden sailing ship with coal-powered steam engines. Shackleton supervised the ship's launching and made sure it was ready to withstand a long ocean journey that included sailing through the pack of sea ice around Antarctica. When he was satisfied with *Discovery*'s performance, he turned his attention to overseeing the loading of what the expedition would need for its planned eighteen-month stay. They would need coal to power the ship's steam engines, special polar clothing, scientific instruments, and hundreds of crates of canned and dried foods. Scott was impressed by Shackleton's enthusiasm to tackle any task that needed doing.

He worked almost nonstop on the preparations. When he had a spare hour or two, Ernest went to see Emily, who lived with her father not far from the expedition offices. Ernest could not stop talking about the expedition. He told Emily he was sure that the journey to Antarctica would bring him fame and fortune.

Emily, on the other hand, had mixed feelings about Ernest and his upcoming adventure. It sounded like a remarkable undertaking. But the expedition was dangerous. Anything could happen. Ernest wouldn't return for nearly two years—if he returned at all. And she wasn't as sure as she had been before that Ernest Shackleton was the man she truly loved.

On July 31, 1901, *Discovery* eased away from the dock in London and sailed down the Thames River, bound for the English coast. The crowd that watched the ship depart—including Ernest's sisters Kathleen, Helen, and Gladys—was abuzz with excitement. So was Ernest. Shackleton realized that he had a good chance to be among the first to reach the South Pole. It was the grand adventure he'd dreamed about since he was a young boy.

Some of the officers and crew of Discovery *pose for a photo on deck before sailing for Antarctica.*

Discovery sailed to the Isle of Wight near England's southern coast. King Edward VII came aboard to give the ship and the expedition a royal send-off. Shackleton cut a dashing figure in his new naval uniform. With Sir Clements's help, he'd received a commission as a sublieutenant in the Royal Naval Reserve.

A few days later, on August 6, *Discovery* headed out into the Atlantic. Emily was there at the dock, waving good-bye. Ernest still did not know whether Emily Dorman would ever be his bride.

Discovery traveled southward along a route that Shackleton knew well from his many years at sea. They sailed down the western coast of Africa, around the Cape of Good Hope, and then east across the Indian Ocean, toward New Zealand.

The men lived together in very cramped quarters, yet Commander Scott insisted that the officers not socialize with the sailors and enlisted men of the expedition. The separation of classes was strong on board *Discovery.*

Shackleton, however, got along well with just about everyone. He quickly befriended Dr. Edward Wilson, the expedition's junior surgeon, who loved poetry as much as Shackleton did. Wilson was also Scott's closest friend on *Discovery*—perhaps his only friend, as Scott kept himself aloof from most of those under his command.

Around midnight on November 28, *Discovery* sailed into the port of Lyttelton on the eastern coast of New Zealand's South Island. Too impatient to wait until morning, Ernest jumped into *Discovery*'s small skiff and rowed to shore. In the village, he went to the postmaster's house

Lyttelton Harbor, New Zealand, about the time DISCOVERY *was docked there in 1901*

and woke him up, demanding any mail that had arrived for *Discovery*'s crew. Among the letters was one addressed to Ernest in tidy handwriting. It was from Emily. Her father had died very unexpectedly, leaving Emily to decide her own future. She wrote that she had made her decision: She wanted to marry Ernest when he returned from the Antarctic. Ernest was happier than he could ever remember being.

In Lyttelton, *Discovery* took on extra food, coal, and other supplies, as well as twenty-three sled dogs.

At the urging of polar explorers from Norway, Scott had reluctantly agreed to take dogs on the expedition. The British idea of the best way to travel in polar regions, however, was not with dogs but by manhauling. Men roped themselves to sledges—the sleds used to transport supplies in the polar regions—and pulled them along behind as they walked. The dogs were loaded onto *Discovery*. But no one aboard knew how to properly harness the dogs or drive them as a team.

Discovery set sail for Antarctica on Christmas Eve 1901. It was midsummer in the Southern Hemisphere. Shackleton watched the green hills of New Zealand gradually disappear behind him. Then the ship was surrounded by ocean. After a week, the first iceberg was spotted, gleaming in the dark water. Soon there were more. Shortly after crossing the Antarctic Circle at 66º30' south latitude, *Discovery* encountered the pack. Ernest had never seen such a sight. Huge flat chunks of drifting ice called floes covered the sea's surface as far as the eye could see. Cautiously, *Discovery* followed a twisted path through the openings, or leads, among the floes. The great pieces of ice groaned and bumped against each other as the ship slid past.

Discovery sailed out of the pack and into the open waters of the Ross Sea four days later. Standing on deck, Ernest got his first look at Antarctica. Beyond the dark water, the continent rose up, white and imposing. To the west he saw the mountains of Victoria Land covered with glaciers that glistened in the sun. *Discovery* sailed on into McMurdo Sound, the southernmost part of the Ross Sea.

On the western side of the sound was Ross Island. Shackleton watched clouds of gas and steam billow from the top of Mount Erebus, the active volcano that formed the highest point on the island.

Scott set a course that took them past Ross Island and along the edge of the Great Ice Barrier (the Barrier). For a week, *Discovery* cruised along this massive wall of ice that rose hundreds of feet straight up from the sea. But the Antarctic winter was approaching. In a few weeks, the temperatures would fall sharply. Then the surface of the sea would begin to freeze, and a ship could become trapped by the rapidly forming ice. On February 1, Scott gave the order for the ship to return to Ross Island. At the southern end of the island, they discovered a small, protected bay at about 78° south latitude. It was a good site for the expedition's winter home. And in the shallow bay, *Discovery* could safely freeze into the sea ice without damage.

Looking southward from Ross Island, there were two large hills—islands, actually—one rocky and black, one snow-clad and white. The men of *Discovery* called them Black Island and White Island. Beyond them was the flat whiteness of the Barrier. Shackleton wrote that the whole place "had a weird and uncanny look."

Once *Discovery* dropped anchor, the crew began preparing the ship for winter. Scott ordered Shackleton to take a small group of men and scope out the path that the "southern party" would take the following spring toward the Pole. Shackleton was honored to be among the first to travel across uncharted Antarctic territory.

He chose Dr. Wilson and the expedition's geologist, Hartley Ferrar, to go with him. On February 19, the three men set out on foot toward White Island.

At midnight on February 20, Shackleton, Wilson, and Ferrar clambered to the top of White Island. To the south, the Great Ice Barrier reached to the horizon. If this was the way to the Pole, Shackleton thought, it didn't look terribly difficult. There were no mountains to climb, as far as they could see. Two days later, the three men were back at *Discovery,* eagerly sharing details of their adventure with the other expedition members. Shackleton had his first taste of leading men across the ice, and he was eager to repeat the experience.

Discovery lies frozen into the sea ice off Hut Point on Ross Island. The hut is in the lower left of the photograph, partially covered by snow drifts.

Winter tightened its grip on Antarctica. By the end of April, the sun disappeared below the horizon. It wouldn't rise again until late August. The weather turned fiercely cold. A thick crust of sea ice formed on the waters of McMurdo Sound. *Discovery* was frozen in place. The men built a tiny wooden hut onshore as a shelter in case something happened to the ship. They called the little piece of land on which it stood Hut Point.

In June, Scott summoned Shackleton to his cabin. He told Shackleton he'd chosen him and Wilson to be his companions in the attempt to reach the South Pole. Shackleton was surprised, but thrilled, to be selected for Scott's southern party. Here was the chance he had been waiting for! He found himself dreaming about Emily and the life they would have once he'd become famous as one of the first men to reach the South Pole.

When spring arrived, the expedition members worked feverishly to get everything ready for the southern party's journey. At the last minute, Scott decided to use the dogs. He put Shackleton in charge of them, even though he didn't know anything about how to handle them.

On November 2, 1902, Scott, Wilson, and Shackleton set off with five sledges heavily loaded with food and supplies. Their main food was pemmican, a fatty meat stew that was high in calories. The men knew they would burn a lot of calories as they trekked across the ice, but they weren't really sure just how much food they would need. Their goal was to reach the South Pole, some eight hundred miles away, and return before winter came again.

Bundled up in polar gear, Shackleton, Scott, and Wilson (LEFT TO RIGHT), set out for the South Pole.

For the first week, a support team carrying additional supplies accompanied the three men. At several points along the way, supplies were buried in the snow for the southern party to eat on their return trip. When the support team turned back, Scott, Shackleton, and Wilson were on their own.

Crossing Antarctica turned out to be far more difficult than the three men had anticipated. The dogs struggled to pull the heavy sledges. Shackleton didn't know it, but he hadn't harnessed the dogs properly. None of the three men knew how to drive them. They stumbled along behind the dogs and the sledges, sinking deeply into the snow with every step.

Slowly they pushed south. Icy winds chilled them to the bone. Their lips and fingers cracked and blistered from frostbite. Every day was the same. Break camp, march all day, set up camp again. By the end of November, the dogs were so weak they could no longer pull their loads alone. So the men harnessed themselves to the sledges and pulled with them.

A week later, more than a month into the journey, Scott announced they were running out of food. To make their food last, they had to cut back their meals drastically. They survived on just a few handfuls of food each day. Hunger became their constant companion. They dreamed about food as they slogged through snow during the day and as they lay shivering in their sleeping bags at night.

After seven weeks, the southern party had gotten only as far as 81° south latitude—only 3° south of where they had started. They calculated their latitude using a sextant and a chronometer (a very accurate type of watch). With the sextant, they determined the position of the sun above the horizon. Knowing the sun's position and the exact time of day, they used nautical tables to figure out their latitude and the distance to the Pole. The South Pole was still several hundred miles away, at 90° south. Shackleton knew they would not make it to the Pole. They had too little food, and their progress was too slow. The dogs were starving, too.

Tension mounted between Scott and Shackleton. Scott became increasingly critical of Shackleton. Shackleton, on the other hand, lost respect for Scott. Scott seemed to be acting with very little concern for their safety, something Shackleton believed a good leader would never do.

When tempers flared, Wilson tried to act as a peacemaker between his two companions.

On December 15, Scott decided that they would stash most of their supplies, including the dog food, and make a "dash" to see if they could reach 82° south in three weeks. He proposed killing the weakest dogs along the way to feed those that remained. With less gear to haul, walking was easier. But they faced another challenge: scurvy. All three men showed some of the early symptoms of the potentially deadly disease. It was caused by a lack of vitamin C in the food they were eating. Their joints ached, their legs swelled, and their gums bled. But Shackleton was the most seriously affected. Along with scurvy, he also had developed a terrible cough.

When Wilson pointed out their swollen legs and bleeding gums to Scott, he assumed their leader would turn back immediately. To Wilson's amazement, Scott insisted they continue marching. Wilson and Shackleton were stunned. After a heated argument, they got Scott to promise they would turn back by December 28, no matter what.

On December 28, they passed 82° south. Going back on his word, Scott told his companions to keep moving. Shackleton could not understand how Scott, as their leader, could deliberately risk their lives. They plodded on, exhausted and starving. On December 30, they reached 82°17' south. They were still four hundred miles from the Pole.

Finally, Scott seemed to realize that they were in a life-or-death situation. On December 31, he agreed to turn back. The three men and the few remaining dogs headed north.

For three weeks, they marched, stopping only to eat tiny meals and catch a few hours of sleep. The last of the dogs died. The three men were constantly hungry and growing weaker every day. Shackleton's cough grew rapidly worse. Once he collapsed in the snow, gasping for breath as sharp pains shot through his chest. Wilson was concerned. But Scott was annoyed and sarcastic, calling Shackleton a burden and "our invalid."

On January 25, they spotted Mount Erebus in the distance. They were roughly sixty miles from Hut Point. But Shackleton was desperately ill. Lying in the tent on the night of January 29, Shackleton overhead Wilson saying that he did not expect Shackleton to survive until morning. But in the morning, Shackleton was still alive. Yet he could barely stand. Despite his protests, Wilson and Scott lifted him onto the sledge. For a while, he rode as his companions pulled and walked. The rest helped him recover, and soon Shackleton could walk again.

A few days later, Scott, Shackleton, and Wilson reached *Discovery.* The terrible ordeal was over.

As the southern party climbed aboard the ship, the other expedition members hardly recognized them. The three men were very thin and had long beards, swollen lips, and peeling faces. Shackleton looked the most ill of all. Everyone noticed the tension between Shackleton and Scott.

From the deck of *Discovery,* Shackleton could see another ship, *Morning,* far out in McMurdo Sound. It was the expedition's relief ship, packed with fresh supplies to equip *Discovery* for the voyage back to England. But *Discovery* was still held firmly in place by thick sea ice.

Members of DISCOVERY's crew assist the returning southern party. Scott came in first, followed closely by Wilson. Shackleton trailed far behind.

Since *Discovery* could not sail, Scott announced that most of the members of the expedition would spend another winter in Antarctica—but not Shackleton. Even though Shackleton was recovering, Scott ordered him to return to England on *Morning*.

On March 1, 1902, Shackleton climbed aboard the ship with a heavy heart. Going home while his expedition comrades remained in Antarctica was an embarrassment.

As the ship sailed out of McMurdo Sound, he stood on deck watching the men who were staying behind gather on Hut Point. Scott was there, too, waving good-bye. He had gotten rid of a man he disliked, and he had a scapegoat for his failure to reach the Pole.

As Shackleton watched Ross Island fade behind a misty veil of falling snow, he vowed to return to Antarctica. He was determined to prove that he was a better explorer than Robert Falcon Scott.

Shackleton was quick to calm anger and encourage laughter. He treated all the men under his command with respect, and in so doing, earned theirs as well. They called Shackleton the Boss.

4

NIMROD

On the long journey home, Ernest Shackleton recovered from his illness. He arrived back in England on June 12, 1903. Emily was overjoyed to see him and full of plans for their wedding. Yet at thirty years old, Ernest had essentially no money and no job. Since he was about to be married, he needed a way to support himself and Emily.

Ernest took a position as a junior editor at the *Royal Magazine* in London. But the salary was so small that he soon quit. Next he tried writing and selling articles about the *Discovery* expedition. He also gave public lectures. With his gift for storytelling, Ernest kept audiences on the edges of their seats. He made a name for himself as a speaker and Antarctic explorer.

Back in England, Shackleton tried several new careers. But he also began planning his return to Antarctica.

But Ernest needed a more permanent job. Several friends recommended him for secretary of the Royal Scottish Geographical Society in Edinburgh, Scotland. When Ernest learned he had gotten the job, he was pleased and relieved. The salary was modest, but it was enough. On April 9, 1904, Ernest and Emily were married in London. They moved to Scotland into a house on the outskirts of Edinburgh.

The newlyweds were quickly accepted into the wealthy and powerful social circles in Edinburgh. Emily was a wonderful hostess, and Ernest came to know many prominent people in business and politics. At first, Ernest tackled his new duties at the geographical society with great enthusiasm. But as the months passed, he grew bored and restless. His thoughts often strayed to Antarctica—the majesty of its glacier-covered mountains and the Great Ice Barrier, the excitement of venturing into its unknown interior. Ernest didn't want to upset Emily, but more than anything he wanted to go back to Antarctica.

In late summer 1904, Robert Falcon Scott and *Discovery* returned to England. Like Shackleton, Scott gave public lectures about the expedition. In his talks, he brought up Shackleton's illness and the fact that he rode on the sledge while Scott and Wilson pulled. It seemed that Scott was trying to make Shackleton look bad in the eyes of the public.

Frustrated with all the attention Scott was getting, Shackleton resigned his position at the geographical society and ran for political office. In the middle of Ernest's campaign for a seat in Parliament, Emily gave birth to their first child, Raymond, on February 2, 1905. When Ernest saw the baby for the first time, he proudly exclaimed that Raymond had "good fists for fighting!" Shackleton was so delighted to have a son that it didn't really bother him when he lost the election.

Later that year, Scott published a book called *The Voyage of the Discovery.* In it, he suggested that it was Shackleton's fault that the southern party hadn't reached the South Pole. Shackleton was furious. He knew the failure was due far more to Scott's poor planning and bad leadership. Scott's twisting of the truth made Shackleton determined to prove that he was the better explorer. He vowed that, somehow, he would get back to Antarctica.

By early 1906, Shackleton had come up with a plan to return to Antarctica and to lead his own expedition to the Pole. The only problem was money. For many months he tried and failed to get the financial backing he needed. Disheartened, he began to think that a second chance at the Pole might never come. He was thirty-two—old for an explorer—and Emily was pregnant with their second child. Perhaps returning to Antarctica was just a dream.

Finally, Shackleton got a break. He had become friends with a wealthy industrialist, William Beardmore, and his wife, Elspeth. Beardmore agreed to loan Shackleton a large sum of money for an expedition. After Beardmore, several more wealthy patrons gave Shackleton enough money to begin.

Full of enthusiasm, Ernest broke the news about the expedition to Emily. She was not happy that her husband was leaving her again for Antarctica. She had her hands full, having just given birth to a little girl, Cecily, in December 1906. By this time, though, Emily knew how bored Ernest was by ordinary jobs and everyday life. She saw that he was happiest when he was planning to go on an expedition. Now that he was about to lead one, he was bursting with energy and optimism. Emily was not about to stand in his way.

In February 1907, Shackleton plunged into preparations for his second journey south. He had just seven months to pull together men and supplies for his British Antarctic Expedition. There was another reason for haste: Scott was planning another expedition, too, although Shackleton guessed his rival would not be prepared to depart until 1908 at the earliest. Shackleton was determined to get there first.

Over the next few months, he assembled his expedition. Four hundred men applied. The fifteen Shackleton chose were an odd assortment of rugged sailors, university professors, amateur naturalists, and gentlemen adventurers.

He selected them more for their personalities than for their experience. Shackleton had learned that getting the right mix of men on an expedition was critical to its success. He asked Frank Wild, who had served aboard *Discovery,* to join the expedition as his second-in-command.

Because dogs had seemed so ineffective to Shackleton in Antarctica, he decided to use Manchurian ponies from China to pull the sledges on his expedition. It was an odd choice, since horses and ponies had proven to be poorly suited for polar travel. But once Shackleton made up his mind, there was no changing it. He also took a motorcar, a gift to the expedition from the Beardmores.

Shackleton oversaw all the details of the preparations. He ordered custom-made windproof clothing. Reindeer-fur sleeping bags and boots were made in Norway. The sledges came from Norway, too. Shackleton selected the food very carefully. It ranged from dried meat and fruits to butter, dried milk, cocoa, and cheese. For the southern party there was pemmican, as well as special protein-rich biscuits that Shackleton had had manufactured to his instructions. Thousands of pounds of supplies—including a camera and motion picture camera—were loaded into 2,500 specially made wooden cases.

Nimrod, the expedition ship, was loaded and ready to sail by the end of July. *Nimrod* was a sailing ship, but it had steam engines to provide power when there was no wind. King Edward VII came aboard to give the expedition a royal send-off. It was a proud moment for Shackleton.

Nimrod set sail on August 7, 1907. When they reached New Zealand, they brought final supplies aboard, including

Ernest Shackleton relaxes on board NIMROD.

the ten Manchurian ponies. At the last minute, Shackleton added nine sled dogs, too. On New Year's Day 1908, more than thirty thousand New Zealanders jammed the docks at Lyttelton to send *Nimrod* on its way. Brass bands played and guns fired salutes. In his cabin, Ernest wrote to Emily, telling her of his hopes and fears for the upcoming expedition. The letters would not be mailed until after the expedition returned to New Zealand, but writing them made Ernest feel closer to Emily, even though they were separated by thousands of miles.

Two weeks later, the ship crossed the Antarctic Circle. With a brisk wind filling its sails, *Nimrod* continued southward, first through the pack ice and then into the Ross Sea.

Nimrod sails carefully through the pack ice surrounding Antarctica.

Shackleton gave orders to sail slowly along the edge of the Great Ice Barrier. He hoped to land on this great sheet of ice and set up a camp. From there he could launch his journey to the Pole. But he couldn't find a place that looked safe enough for a landing. Not willing to take unnecessary risks with the lives of his men, Shackleton headed for the familiar territory of Ross Island.

The island looked much as Shackleton remembered it, with towering Mount Erebus puffing steam and smoke. He chose Cape Royds, a rocky point of land several miles north of Hut Point, as the site for the expedition camp.

By February 22, 1908, all the supplies and equipment had been unloaded—not a day too soon, as the sea surface was beginning to freeze. *Nimrod* turned and steamed north. It would return the following year. Shackleton believed there was no point in keeping a ship in Antarctica through the winter. It was useless and at the mercy of the sea ice. Instead, he and his men would spend the winter in a hut built to house them all. Shackleton and the fifteen other members of the expedition watched *Nimrod* gradually disappear over the horizon. They were alone in Antarctica.

It took a few days to store all the supplies and to erect the hut that would be the expedition's home for the next year. When the work was done, Shackleton chose six men to climb Mount Erebus. After reaching the top of the volcano, they returned to the hut five days later. Just weeks after arriving, Shackleton's expedition had already made history, becoming the first to climb an Antarctic peak.

After conquering Mount Erebus, the men settled in for the long, dark winter. The hut was small and cramped. Shackleton worked hard to create harmony among his men. There were no barriers based on rank. Shackleton was quick to calm anger and encourage laughter. He treated all the men under his command with respect and, in so doing, earned theirs as well. They called Shackleton the Boss.

In June 1908, Shackleton chose Frank Wild, his second-in-command; Eric Marshall, the expedition doctor; and meteorologist Jameson Adams to join him as part of the southern party. In late August, all the members of the expedition helped move supplies twenty miles to Hut Point—the starting point for the journey.

Only four ponies had survived the ocean voyage and the long Antarctic winter. Shackleton knew four ponies could not pull the sledges all by themselves. He rejected the idea of taking the dogs. And the motorcar traveled only eight miles before becoming stuck in a shallow drift of snow. Shackleton resigned himself to the fact that he and his companions would be manhauling sledges over the frozen surface, as he had done years before with Scott.

Shackleton left instructions with the men staying at Cape Royds about what to do if the southern party did not return as planned. First, they were to send out a search party. If by March 1 there was no sign of the southern party, they were to assume all four men were dead and return to New Zealand on *Nimrod,* which was scheduled to come back around the end of January 1909.

On November 3, Shackleton, Wild, Marshall, and Adams set out from Hut Point for the South Pole. The four horses—Grisi, Socks, Quan, and Chinaman—were each harnessed to a sledge. Packed on the sledges was ninety-one days' supply of food for the men as well as fodder for the horses.

At first the ponies pulled well. But the bitter cold, fierce wind, and great strain of dragging sledges over deep snow and rough ice was very hard on the shaggy beasts. Chinaman was the first to die, followed by Grisi and Quan. Only tough little Socks survived. As they lost the ponies, Shackleton and his companions tied themselves to the sledges and pulled. Their progress slowed. Shackleton could see that at the rate they were going their

The ponies are hitched to the sledges as Shackleton, Wild, Marshall, and Adams begin their journey southward toward the Pole.

supplies would not last as long as he had planned. They did eat the meat of the unfortunate ponies, but it was not enough. To make their food supply last, they had to cut back on the amount of food they ate each day.

Shackleton knew the first part of the route, which he had traveled with Scott and Wilson six years earlier. Then, on November 25, they passed 82°17' south latitude—Scott's record for furthest south. What lay beyond was unknown.

A few days later, they spotted a range of high mountains in the distance—the Transantarctic Mountains. The closer the men got, the more formidable the mountains looked. Was there a pass through those jagged peaks? Shackleton wondered. He didn't know, but he was confident they would find one.

After several days of climbing, Shackleton and his companions found themselves looking up at an enormous glacier that stretched out in front of them like a giant highway of ice. They had found a pass through the mountains. The glacier looked like it might lead to the Pole. But what a terrifying path it was. The ice was riddled with deep cracks, called crevasses. It was as slippery as glass. Socks had a terrible time. He could not grip the ice with his small hooves, so the men used their ice axes to cut steps for him.

The four men and their pony detoured around every crevasse they could see. But many were hidden under thin crusts of snow. Each man put a foot into a crevasse many times a day, always catching himself before sliding in all the way. It was terrifyingly dangerous. But the Boss led them on with calm determination.

Then, on December 7, as they moved along single-file, Wild, who was at the end of the line leading Socks, suddenly shouted for help. The others turned to see him clawing at the edge of a crevasse. Grabbing hold of Wild, they pulled him to safety. Breathlessly, they peered into the crevasse. Socks had vanished down a crack so deep they couldn't see the bottom.

Shackleton and his men continued up the glacier, dragging a thousand pounds of food, fuel, and equipment by themselves. They were climbing noticeably in altitude, which they measured with a hypsometer. They reached seven thousand feet above sea level, then eight, then nine.

They stretched out their food supply, trying to make seven days of rations last ten. On Christmas Day, they were still 250 miles from the Pole. To increase their chances of making it all the way, they cut their rations even more.

They marched on, climbing steadily. Shackleton guessed that the Pole lay on a high, icy plateau. On December 28, they left the glacier behind and strode onto a flat plain. A steady, breathlessly cold wind blew. It seemed to be coming from the Pole itself. The temperature was many degrees below zero. At the end of each day's march, they pitched their thin tent, ate their small meal, and crawled into their cold sleeping bags, which were stiff with ice. The cold was becoming unbearable, and they were nearing eleven thousand feet above sea level. The high altitude bothered them all, but it was especially hard on the Boss. He often found himself gasping for breath.

On January 3, 1909, they reached 87°22' south. With 158 miles to go, Shackleton suggested they leave most of their gear and make one final dash. The others agreed. The next day they set out, marching as fast as they could.

But on January 6, Shackleton realized they were all too exhausted to continue. Rather than risk the lives of his men, he decided to turn back. It was one of the hardest decisions of his life. All his dreams depended on reaching the Pole: fame, money enough so his family could live well, and proof that he could do what Scott could not.

For two days, a blizzard trapped the four men in their tent. Then on January 9, they walked together to a point where Marshall took a reading of the sun's position with the sextant to determine their final latitude. They had reached 88°23' south, just ninety-seven miles from the Pole. After planting a flag in the snow, they took pictures of each other.

That night in his journal, Shackleton wrote, "We have done our best."

The return trip was a race with death. Their survival hinged on finding every reserve of food that they had buried in the snow along the long, dangerous path back to Ross Island. If they missed just one, they would starve to death. Their feet were numb, and their faces and hands were blistered and bleeding from frostbite. But they marched as hard and fast as they could, trying to make twenty miles a day. On January 16, the Transantarctic Mountains loomed up on the horizon. On January 20, they reached the top of the great glacier. But that evening, Shackleton collapsed, coughing and fighting for breath. Marshall checked Shackleton's pulse.

Adams, Wild, and Shackleton (LEFT TO RIGHT) stand beside the British flag just ninety-seven miles from the Pole. Marshall took the photograph.

It was weak and irregular. His strange illness had returned. But the next day, he recovered enough to travel. After that, he steadily improved.

On January 26, the men ate the last of the food they carried. The next site where they had buried supplies was still twenty miles off. The following day, first Wild, then Adams, and finally Shackleton collapsed from exhaustion. Summoning all his strength, Marshall pushed ahead alone. Again and again, he put a leg into a crevasse, always managing to catch himself before falling in. Marshall reached the supplies, grabbed some food, and hurried back to his starving companions.

On February 13, back on the Barrier, they still had 230 miles to go. Shackleton kept them moving. Outwardly, he was calm and confident. On the inside, he was worried. Time was running out. If the southern party was not back by March 1, Shackleton knew his men would follow his orders, and the ship would sail back to New Zealand.

On February 27, with Ross Island on the horizon, Marshall collapsed and couldn't go on. Adams, too, was very ill. Shackleton knew their situation was desperate. In forty-eight hours, *Nimrod* would sail. He ordered Adams and Marshall to stay put. Grabbing a bit of food, Shackleton and Wild started walking as fast as they could.

At eight o'clock the next evening, Wild and Shackleton reached the hut at Hut Point. They found a note—*Nimrod* had returned, but it might sail from Cape Royds before the end of the month. Was the ship already gone? Shackleton wondered. Had they been abandoned? Exhausted, the Boss and Wild huddled in the cold hut to wait for morning.

Weathered and weary, Wild, Shackleton, Marshall, and Adams (LEFT TO RIGHT) stand on NIMROD'S deck. In 128 days, they had covered 1,700 miles.

The next day, March 1, Wild and Shackleton spotted a ship coming toward Hut Point. Madly, they waved a flag to catch the crew's attention. Having given up the southern party for dead, *Nimrod* had been set to sail north, but some of Shackleton's men had persuaded the ship's captain to swing past Hut Point for one last look. They were rescued!

Shackleton had not slept for fifty-four hours. But he insisted on leading the rescue party that went back to pick up Adams and Marshall. By March 4, all of his men were safely on board. Shackleton gave the order, and *Nimrod* steamed north.

Shackleton came up with a daring plan. He proposed to cross the continent from one coast to the other. His idea was to sail down through the Weddell Sea and land a party of men on the continent.

5

ENDURANCE

On June 14, 1909, Ernest Shackleton returned from Antarctica to a hero's welcome. A crowd of ten thousand people met him when he arrived in London. He became famous almost overnight. Knighted by the king for his daring and accomplishments, he became Sir Ernest Shackleton. Emily became Lady Shackleton. She was pleased to have Ernest home again, and she enjoyed basking in the limelight with her husband.

Shackleton wasted no time in capitalizing on his sudden popularity. He set off on lecture tours, giving hundreds of talks in England and Europe. As he retold the story of the expedition, he showed photographs—large black-and-white slides that were projected using a machine called a magic lantern. Shackleton also showed a motion picture.

Like the slides, it was in black-and-white, but the moving pictures allowed people to experience Antarctica as never before.

Less than six months after returning to England, Shackleton published a book about the expedition called *The Heart of the Antarctic.* It immediately became a bestseller. In his book, Shackleton generously praised the men who had been with him on the expedition. He believed that good leadership meant giving credit to the men under his command. After all, they too had faced Antarctica's challenges.

All of this success, however, did not make Shackleton a rich man. He was deeply in debt. The money from William Beardmore and other patrons had not covered all the expedition's expenses. All the profits from sales of Shackleton's book and from his lectures went to paying off his debts. But it wasn't enough.

Men wearing fur polar gear promote one of Shackleton's public lectures in 1909.

When members of the British government learned about his financial predicament, they arranged for Shackleton to receive a large sum of money as a reward for his polar accomplishments. With it, he paid off most of his bills.

In September 1909, Robert Falcon Scott announced plans to return to Antarctica and again try to reach the South Pole. Each bit of news Shackleton heard about Scott's upcoming expedition made him long to go back to Antarctica. After two expeditions, Shackleton knew he wasn't in perfect health, although he publicly denied having any physical problems. He also refused to let a doctor examine him.

In July 1910, Scott's expedition was ready to depart. Shackleton went to see Scott off at the dock and to wish him well. Shackleton assumed, as most people did, that Scott would be the first to reach the South Pole. After all, Shackleton and his men had found the path and had essentially shown the way. But in October came startling news. Roald Amundsen, a Norwegian explorer who had led the world to believe he was going to the Arctic, announced that he was heading south instead. Amundsen was going to try to beat Scott to the South Pole. The whole world waited for news, wondering which of the two men would be the one to claim the prize.

While Amundsen and Scott were racing to the Pole, Ernest grew increasingly restless and unhappy in England. In May 1911, he and Emily and their two children moved to Putney Heath, a fashionable suburb of London. Two months later, Emily gave birth to their second son, Edward Alexander Shackleton. But Ernest and Emily were not getting along well. Although he adored his children,

In the years following the Nimrod *expedition, Ernest and Emily grew apart. Emily's life revolved around their children. Ernest's focus was Antarctica.*

Ernest spent less and less time at home. He kept busy with various investment schemes, although none of them was successful. His mind was on Antarctica. He was burning with curiosity about what was happening there.

Both Scott and Amundsen set out for the Pole in the Antarctic spring of 1911, England's autumn. Scott started from Cape Evans, a site on Ross Island between Cape Royds and Hut Point. Amundsen began from a camp on the Great Ice Barrier, in a place called the Bay of Whales. Scott chose to travel with a mix of ponies, motor sledges, and dogs but ended up manhauling his sledges once again. Amundsen's party, on the other hand, skied behind sledges pulled by well-trained and expertly handled dog teams. Amundsen reached the South Pole first, almost easily, on December 14, 1911.

Scott reached the Pole five weeks later, only to find a Norwegian flag and a note from Amundsen. Bitterly disappointed, Scott and his four companions started back. They were caught in a blizzard not far from Ross Island and were trapped in their tents for days. Desperately short of food and fuel, they froze to death. News of the tragedy didn't reach the outside world until early in 1912.

The news stunned Shackleton. But it immediately set him to thinking: since the Pole had been reached, what was left to accomplish in Antarctica? Shackleton came up with a daring plan. He proposed to cross the continent from one coast to the other. His idea was to sail down through the Weddell Sea and land a party of men on the continent. They would travel to the South Pole and from there to Ross Island, where they would be met by a relief party that would travel to Antarctica on a second ship, *Aurora.*

In 1912 Scott arrived at the South Pole only to discover that Amundsen's Norwegian expedition had beaten him by only several weeks.

The relief party was responsible for traveling inland and for laying down food for Shackleton and his men to pick up on their way across the continent. Shackleton's Imperial Transantarctic Expedition, as he called it, would be "the last great polar journey . . . greater than the journey to the Pole and back."

Shackleton was fiercely determined to mount this new expedition. As in the past, the first difficult task he faced was to raise funding to pay for it. The British government provided some money, and a wealthy Scottish industrialist, Sir James Caird, made a very large donation. By the end of December 1913, Shackleton had enough money to hire men for the expedition and to buy equipment, supplies, and a ship. The ship was *Polaris,* a very strong wooden ship built to withstand the battering of heavy floes in pack ice. Shackleton changed the ship's name to *Endurance.*

For this expedition, Shackleton decided to take sled dogs—and to learn how to handle them properly to pull the sledges. He took great care in choosing all the supplies, from tents and clothes to sledging rations. Even more care went into selecting the men who would go with him. Once again he asked Frank Wild to be his second-in-command. Wild accepted immediately. For captain of *Endurance,* he chose Frank Worsley, a New Zealander who had a reputation as an outstanding navigator. Shackleton convinced an Australian photographer named Frank Hurley to sign on as the expedition's cameraman and George Marston as its artist. There were two surgeons—James McIlroy and Alexander Macklin—several scientists, and more than a dozen ship's officers and crew.

As Shackleton assembled his crew and fitted out *Endurance,* political unrest was building in Europe. There was talk of war. Tensions between governments grew daily. There was tension between Emily and Ernest, too. Emily was not happy that Ernest was heading off on yet another expedition. But she knew there was nothing she could do. Their marriage was not as happy as she had hoped it would be. Emily and Ernest had come to lead increasingly separate lives. Emily's life centered on their children. Ernest's was focused on Antarctica. Although Ernest loved to be with his children, he could not resist the pull of exploration. He realized his shortcomings as a father and husband. In a letter to Emily, he wrote "I am just good as an explorer and nothing else."

Endurance sailed down the Thames River toward the English coast on August 1, 1914. That same day, Germany declared war on France, and World War I began. Shackleton sent a telegram to the British Admiralty, volunteering *Endurance* and all aboard for the war effort. A telegram quickly came in reply. It contained just one word: Proceed.

One week later, *Endurance* left England for South America. In Buenos Aires, Argentina, sixty-nine burly sled dogs were loaded on board. Kennels had been built for them around the edges of the ship's main deck.

In early November, *Endurance* arrived at Grytviken, one of several small whaling stations on South Georgia Island, east of Cape Horn. The whalers, who hunted whales in the Weddell Sea, told Shackleton that the pack ice there had not broken up yet that spring.

Endurance follows a lead of open water through the maze of ice floes in the pack.

They advised him to delay the expedition's departure for a month. Shackleton was anxious to reach Antarctica, but he took their advice.

On December 5, 1914, *Endurance* left South Georgia Island. Six days later, the ship entered the pack in the Weddell Sea. For six weeks, Captain Worsley, who had never seen pack ice, piloted *Endurance* carefully through the maze of floes, following narrow leads of open water among them.

The pack changed constantly as winds and currents stirred the jumbled pieces of ice. Sometimes seals bobbed up like furry corks in the open water of the leads. Penguins rocketed out of the sea onto floes. Always curious, they would waddle over to the ship and stare as it sailed past.

In early January 1915, the men sighted land. For a few days, the ship steamed along the one-hundred-foot-high wall of barrier ice that marked the edge of the Antarctic continent. Shackleton thought they would soon reach the place where he wanted to land if the weather held.

But the weather didn't hold. The winds shifted, nudging the floes ever tighter around the ship. There were fewer and fewer leads for *Endurance* to follow. By mid-January, there were no leads at all. The floes were freezing together, forming a solid mass of ice around the ship. Gradually, the seriousness of their situation dawned on Shackleton and the men under his command. *Endurance* was trapped in the pack. Like a fly caught in some giant frozen spiderweb, the ship couldn't escape.

For several more weeks, the crew held out hope that the pack would break up and that they could batter their way to open water. But the pack ice didn't break up. Shackleton accepted their fate and ordered the fires that powered the ship's steam engines put out. *Endurance* was stuck in a sea of ice, completely at the mercy of the drifting pack.

Shackleton was bitterly disappointed. It looked as if he wouldn't be able to make the Imperial Transantarctic Expedition. But in front of his men, Shackleton didn't show the slightest glimmer of disappointment, anger, or frustration. The only thing that mattered was to get all the members of the expedition safely back to civilization. Doing so was his responsibility. No one in the world knew exactly where *Endurance* was, so no one would be coming to rescue them. They would have to rescue themselves.

Shackleton assembled the men. In a quiet, matter-of-fact way, he explained their situation and the dangers they faced. Winter was coming, but he assured them they would survive it. The currents in the Weddell Sea moved clockwise. They were carrying the pack ice—and *Endurance*—slowly north and a bit west, toward the Antarctic Peninsula. Shackleton told his men that in the spring they might travel over the sea ice to reach land. Or they could stay with the ship. As the weather warmed, the pack would break up and release them, and they'd sail home. Satisfied with the Boss's calm explanations, the men busied themselves getting *Endurance* ready for the long, dark winter ahead.

Out on the ice around the ship, the men used blocks of ice to build kennels for the dogs. The kennels looked like the igloos built in the Arctic. So the men called them dogloos.

Dogs stand outside their dogloos on the ice near Endurance.

Members of ENDURANCE*'s crew warm themselves in front of the ship's roaring stove on a bitterly cold winter night.*

Even as winter bore down on them and the weather got worse, the dogs didn't seem to mind the cold. They simply curled up in their dogloos or burrowed into drifts of soft snow.

Shackleton knew that the survival of his men largely depended on their keeping busy and never giving in to despair. The dogs were wonderful companions. They were divided into six teams, and each team was assigned to a group of men. The men played with the dogs and held races and competitions. They also took the dogs along to hunt seals, an important source of food for both dogs and men.

On May 1, 1915, the sun disappeared below the horizon. Darkness closed in around the ship. *Endurance* became a tiny haven of light and warmth in an immense sea of ice. While the winter winds howled, the men sat around the ship's stove and played cards and chess.

They read books, kept journals, held sing-alongs, and put on skits. Some studied the stars and the weather. Others drilled holes through the ice and snared fish from the water below. Shackleton was always encouraging his men, keeping their minds on their activities rather than on possible problems they might face.

Weeks turned into months, and winter slowly passed. The pack continued to drift north by northwest, taking *Endurance* with it. As long as the pack stayed solid, Shackleton knew the ship was relatively safe. But as spring approached, the pack began to move around them. Under great pressure from currents and wind, the ice was compressed until it could stand the strain no more. The pack began to crack and buckle. Creaking and groaning, enormous slabs of ice piled up along fractures in the pack.

The ice pressed harder and harder on *Endurance.* Day and night, the men listened to it bump and grind against the hull. Shackleton knew *Endurance* was strongly built, but he doubted it was strong enough to survive this crushing pressure. "The ship can't live in this, Skipper," he said quietly to Worsley one day. "What the ice gets, the ice keeps."

Gradually, *Endurance* began to lose the battle with the pack. Its rudder cracked. By September, the pressure was so great that the massive walls of the ship's hull were being forced inward, bending door frames and causing the huge crossbeams to buckle. Leaks appeared. The ship's carpenter, Harry McNeish, worked tirelessly to plug them.

On October 24, *Endurance* suddenly shook violently and tilted hard to the right. Shackleton scrambled overboard,

ENDURANCE tips over to one side as the pack tightens its grip around the ship's hull.

his pulse racing. He could see that the ice was pressing so hard that the ship was bending and twisting under the pressure. The moving ice tore part of the stern away. *Endurance* started leaking badly.

While McNeish tried to repair the damage, the men feverishly gathered supplies, clothing, sledging gear, and dog food and moved it off the ship and onto the ice. Worsley dashed through the library, tearing maps and charts out of books. Above his head, thick wooden beams cracked and splintered.

For the next two days, the men of *Endurance* tried to save their ship. But on October 27, the ice suddenly contracted again. The decks splintered. Water began to pour into the hold. At five o'clock in the evening, the Boss gave the order to abandon ship. The men lowered the lifeboats down onto the ice. One by one, they helped the dogs to safety. Then they stood back, numb with cold and shock, and watched *Endurance* being crushed. Shackleton was the last to leave. He hoisted the ship's flag, and the men on the ice gave three cheers. But there was little to cheer about. The members of the Imperial Transantarctic Expedition were homeless and adrift on the sea ice.

One of the dog teams looks on as ENDURANCE sinks farther below the ice.

The greatest threat to their survival was fear. Shackleton had to keep the men calm, their spirits high, and their minds focused on a goal. The goal was clear: they had to reach land.

6

OCEAN CAMP AND PATIENCE CAMP

Bewildered and shivering, the men pitched their tents a few dozen yards from the crushed ship that had been their home on the ice. While his men tried to sleep, Shackleton paced back and forth, his mind racing. The greatest threat to their survival was fear. Shackleton had to keep the men calm, their spirits high, and their minds focused on a goal.

The goal was clear: they had to reach land. Shackleton knew there was a hut and supplies—left for shipwrecked sailors—on Paulet Island, a tiny dot of land near the top of the Antarctic Peninsula. But Paulet Island was some 350 miles away.

Harnessed together like sled dogs, members of the crew struggle to pull one of the lifeboats across the ice.

The next morning, Shackleton assembled his men. As always, he showed no panic or pessimism. He simply said that since the ship was crushed, they would go home. Then he laid out his plan. They would travel on foot across the sea ice toward Paulet Island, dragging the lifeboats, sledges, and supplies with the help of the dogs. Crossing the rough surface of the pack, Shackleton explained, would be hard going. They had to travel as lightly as possible. Each man could take just two pounds of personal gear. Shackleton set the example by emptying his pockets of coins and tossing his gold watch onto the snow.

After a few days' rest, they set out on October 30. The men harnessed the dogs to the sledges. They harnessed themselves to the lifeboats. Heavily loaded, the boats each weighed thousands of pounds. Men and dogs struggled and strained over the rough, broken ice and wet snow, pulling with all their might. But at the end of an exhausting day, they had covered just a single mile.

After two more days of the same backbreaking, muscle-tearing work, Shackleton called a halt. At the pace they were traveling, it would take them a year to reach land. They were still close enough to *Endurance* to see it clearly in the distance. Dragging the lifeboats over the sharp ice was damaging them, too. Without the boats, they could not survive.

Once again Shackleton called his men together. They would find a large, solid floe, he said, set up a more permanent camp, and simply wait for the pack to break up. When it did, they would launch the lifeboats and row to land. A suitable floe was found nearby, and the men poured their remaining energy into creating a new home on the ice. They called it Ocean Camp.

Life at Ocean Camp quickly fell into a routine. It was spring, and the men enjoyed twenty-four hours of daylight. The temperatures, while still cold, were usually above zero. Each day started with a breakfast of fried seal meat, biscuits, and hot tea prepared on a stove Hurley had made that burned seal blubber as fuel. Then the men did chores around camp or went hunting for seals to supplement the food they had saved from *Endurance.* Lunch was served at one o'clock. During the afternoons, Shackleton let his men read, exercise the dogs, play cards—whatever would keep their minds off their fears. Directly after dinner, most of the men crawled into their sleeping bags.

Shackleton (FAR LEFT) stands next to Wild at Ocean Camp. Other members of the crew are in the background, along with piles of supplies salvaged from ENDURANCE.

Days stretched into weeks. Spring turned to summer. After dinner on November 21, Shackleton happened to look toward *Endurance*. What was left of the ship was sinking. The Boss gave a shout and his men came running. Silently they stood together, watching the broken vessel slip from sight beneath the ice. "She's gone, boys," Shackleton said softly.

As temperatures rose, the surface of the pack began to melt and get mushy. Some of the floes around Ocean Camp began to separate. Narrow leads of open water appeared. The pack was loosening. But it still showed no signs of breaking up enough to launch the lifeboats.

December arrived, and with it bad storms with high winds. The winds churned the loosening pieces of sea ice, causing them to grind and bump against one another.

Hurley took this photograph of the splintered remains of ENDURANCE a few days before the wreck sank completely.

Battered by neighboring chunks, the floe Ocean Camp sat on began growing noticeably smaller as its edges were ground away.

Every day, Worsley calculated their position. He discovered that they were drifting generally northwest at a rate of about two miles per day. But some days the pack seemed to move east, away from land. Shackleton knew what this change in direction meant. They were reaching the top of the Weddell Sea, where the currents in their clockwise spiral began heading eastward. Shackleton was worried—they might be moving farther from land. Should they stay where they were and hope the pack would break up soon? he wondered. Or should they try again to drag themselves and their gear toward land?

As Christmas 1915 approached, Shackleton made a decision. They would pack up and travel toward Paulet Island, he told his men, after having an early Christmas dinner on December 22. On December 23, they headed westward. But the surface of the floes was so soft that the men sank to their knees in wet slush with almost every step. By the end of the first day, they had covered less than a mile. Their progress was even worse on the days that followed. Shackleton sensed his men were growing restless and discouraged. On December 27, McNeish, the carpenter, refused to go on. Since *Endurance* had sunk, he said, his duty to obey orders had ended.

Shackleton remained calm. If they were to survive, he had to keep his men together, and they had to respect his authority. In a quiet voice, Shackleton read out the ship's regulations, which stated that the men were bound by law to obey him until the expedition—not just the ship—reached a safe port. Grudgingly, McNeish acknowledged he was right.

Two days later, Shackleton called a halt to the dreadful march. It was pointless. Wearily, the men pitched their tents and unpacked their gear. They named their new home on the ice Patience Camp.

New Year's Day 1916 came and went. Their supplies of food retrieved from *Endurance* were dwindling. Seals were scarce, too. As the food shortage became more critical, Shackleton realized they could no longer feed the dogs and themselves. With a heavy heart, he ordered that they begin shooting the dogs. Dog meat would become food for the men. The task fell to Wild, who described it as the worst job he'd ever had in his life.

On January 21, Worsley announced that they had drifted north of the Antarctic Circle. They were 150 miles from the nearest land. But still the pack showed no sign of breaking up. Shackleton hardly slept. He worried about their vanishing food supply, the drift of the pack, and the approaching winter. Already the temperature was dropping. Each day, the sun spiraled lower in the sky, a reminder of the coming winter darkness. But most of all, Shackleton worried about the health and safety of his men. Yet he hid his worries well. On the surface he was always the optimist. His attitude instilled confidence in the men. They believed that somehow, no matter how bad things got, the Boss would get them safely home.

Early in March, the floe that Patience Camp sat on began to move up and down. The motion was slight at first.

But to a group of sailors, it was unmistakable: their chunk of ice was riding ocean swells. At last, they were nearing the edge of the pack! Excitement rippled through camp as Shackleton ordered everyone to practice loading and launching the boats. The moment they reached open water, they had to be ready to leap into the boats.

The ocean swells got stronger. All around Patience Camp, the floes began to move, first separating, then smashing together again. The first day of winter arrived on March 21. On March 23, the men sighted land, the first they had seen in sixteen months. But it was not Paulet Island, as they had hoped. It was Joinville Island, which lay north of Paulet Island. Strong currents had been sweeping them northward with greater speed than they had realized.

On March 30, the remaining dogs were shot and eaten. The ice still held the men prisoners. But they knew freedom was coming. As the ocean swells grew stronger still, big chunks of their floe cracked off. Their base camp was disappearing under their feet. On April 9, Shackleton ordered the boats made ready and had the men take down their tents and break camp. They all ate lunch standing up—they had to be ready to jump into the boats at a moment's notice.

An hour later, Shackleton gave the order the men had been longing to hear: All hands into the boats! The men piled into the three lifeboats and pushed them into the frigid water.

Crashing waves gave way to huge swells that came at them one after another. First the boat would be swept up one side of a swell, and then hurled at great speed down the other side.

7

JAMES CAIRD

The lifeboats plunged into a maze of broken floes. Heavy swells churned the pack, sending great chunks of ice smashing and splintering against each other. Time and again, jagged slabs lurched dangerously close to the boats. Each time, the men leaned into the oars with all their might and slipped out of harm's way with just inches to spare.

Shackleton was in charge of *James Caird,* the largest of the three lifeboats. Captain Worsley commanded *Dudley Docker.* Hubert Hudson, navigator of *Endurance,* was at the helm of the smallest boat, *Stancomb Wills.* Standing in *James Caird,* Shackleton shouted encouragement to the men in the other boats, urging them to stay together.

For hours they rowed, fighting waves and dodging floes. At sunset, Shackleton could see the men were exhausted. Before the light faded completely from the sky, he spotted a floe that looked large enough to hold them all. They rowed to it, drew up the boats, and set up camp on its slushy surface.

But Shackleton was too worried about their situation to sleep. Fearing their heaving floe might break up while the men slept, he had some of the crew keep watch. Sure enough, in the middle of the night, the floe suddenly split. The guard shouted an alarm. Shackleton leaped out of his tent in time to see the crack open directly beneath another tent. The men inside scrambled to get out. But one crewman, Ernest Holmes, still in his sleeping bag, slipped through the crack into the icy water. Quick as lightning, Shackleton reached down, grabbed the sinking man, and pulled him back up onto the floe.

At dawn on the second day, the men were back in the boats. They rowed hard while the helmsman on each boat worked frantically to steer through the floes. The waves grew larger. Every few minutes, icy spray soaked the men. Slowly but surely, the three boats approached the edge of the pack. Beyond the floes they could see open water. They pulled harder at the oars, eager to be free of the ice that had held them for so many months. The moment came—the boats cleared the pack!

Relief turned to dismay as great waves crashed into the little boats, threatening to swamp them. Shackleton ordered a retreat. Their chances of survival were better among the ice floes.

They rowed westward until sunset, and then camped on another floe. Most of the men slept. But Shackleton kept watch throughout the night.

A heavy snowfall kept them trapped on the floe much of the next day. Late in the afternoon, they took to the boats once again. But darkness soon forced them to stop. They searched for a floe sturdy enough for a camp. But none was to be found. Trying to sound as encouraging as he could, Shackleton told the men they would have to sleep in the boats. After a day of battling the waves, the men were soaked with saltwater and frightfully cold. All through the night they sat huddled together, listening to the thump of floes and the explosive, hissing breath of the killer whales that circled the boats in the darkness.

On the morning of the fourth day, Shackleton could see the strain starting to show on the faces of his men. Many were seasick. They were all extremely thirsty, for they had little water left to drink. He ordered the boats to a sturdy-looking floe long enough for the cook to make a hot meal. Then it was back to rowing again. For a few minutes, the sun came out—long enough for Worsley to take a sighting and figure out their position. Keeping his voice low, so the men could not overhear their conversation, Worsley told Shackleton they were thirty miles *east* of Patience Camp. Despite rowing for three days, the current had carried them backward, away from land. Without a trace of disappointment showing on his face, the Boss turned to the men and said simply that they "had not done as well as expected."

All the rest of the day, they rowed. They spent a second night in the boats. During the night, the temperature dropped below zero. In the morning, the men discovered their saltwater-soaked clothing had frozen solid, like armor.

At dawn on April 13, their fifth day at sea, Shackleton quietly took stock of his men. All were terribly dehydrated, with cracked lips and swollen tongues. Some were very ill. He feared they would die if he did not get them to land soon.

The wind shifted, blowing hard from the southeast. The sudden change in the weather gave Shackleton hope. With the wind at their backs, the men rowed with all their might toward the tip of the Antarctic Peninsula. Late in the day, two tiny points of land appeared on the horizon: Clarence Island and, beyond it, Elephant Island. Shackleton knew those two islands were their last hope for survival. They had to reach one or the other—or face certain death in the open ocean beyond.

They spent a third night in the boats. During the night, the current carried them north of Clarence Island. Elephant Island was their last hope. On the morning of the sixth day, Shackleton stood in the bow of *James Caird* and spoke encouragingly to his exhausted men. They had to reach land, he told them. His confidence inspired them. With trembling, frozen hands, the men grabbed the oars and rowed with the last of their strength.

By midafternoon they were just ten miles away from Elephant Island. They could see its craggy, snowcapped peaks. But as they got closer to the island, strong currents pushed them back out to sea. By sunset they still had not gotten close enough to land. Not wanting to attempt landing on the island's rocky coast in the darkness, Shackleton decided they must wait until dawn to make another attempt.

Stancomb Wills was taking on water—so much water that Shackleton ordered it tied to *James Caird* with a rope for safety. During the night, swirling snowflakes hid the boats from each other. When the snow stopped, Shackleton saw to his horror that *Dudley Docker* was gone.

Sick with worry for Worsley and the men with him, Shackleton waited anxiously for the light of day. But when the sun came up, a thick mist filled the air. He couldn't see more than a few yards in any direction.

Out of the mist came the sound of waves breaking onto rock. There was Elephant Island! During the night, the currents had changed. The boats had been carried close to shore.

After 497 days of drifting at the mercy of the sea, the rocky shore of Elephant Island was a welcome sight for Shackleton and his men.

Filled with hope and fear, the men in the two boats rowed along the rocky coast, looking for a place to land. A narrow beach came into view. But huge boulders were in front of it. Shackleton watched the waves crashing against the rocks. Could they avoid being smashed against those boulders and make it to shore? It was a long shot. But Shackleton knew he had no choice but to try. He and his men had been without water for forty-eight hours. They would either reach land or die trying.

Just as the men were bracing themselves to row as hard as they could for the beach, *Dudley Docker* came into view. Enormously relieved, Shackleton gave the order to row for shore. With their last reserves of strength, the men powered the boats past the rocks and onto the beach. For the first time in more than sixteen months, Ernest Shackleton and the men of *Endurance* stood on cold, hard ground.

The ravenously hungry men killed several seals that were on the beach and were soon feasting on sizzling seal steaks. With full stomachs, many of the men spread out their sleeping bags on the rocky ground and fell asleep. Others sat around the fire, slowly relaxing from their seven-day ordeal in the lifeboats. Shackleton had not slept since they had left Patience Camp. Knowing that for the moment his men were safe, he allowed himself to sleep for a few hours.

Shackleton woke realizing that Elephant Island was not the answer to their problems. The island wasn't regularly visited by whalers or anyone else. They were still stranded. Someone had to go for help.

A few days later, Shackleton laid out his plan. He and five others would sail *James Caird* to South Georgia Island, which lay eight hundred miles to the northeast—luckily in the same direction as the ocean currents. At a whaling station on South Georgia, they would get a ship and return to rescue the men left on Elephant Island. The men were stunned. Cross eight hundred miles of the worst ocean in the world in a battered twenty-two-foot lifeboat? Most of them thought the journey Shackleton proposed was nothing short of impossible. On the other hand, if anyone could do it, it would be the Boss!

To accompany him to South Georgia, Shackleton chose Captain Worsley, the carpenter McNeish, and sailors Tom Crean, Tim McCarthy, and John Vincent. Frank Wild was left in charge of the men on Elephant Island.

Over the next few days, using materials scavenged from the other two lifeboats, McNeish built up the sides of *James Caird* and constructed a wood-and-canvas covering over part of its open top. The men loaded the little boat with a four-week supply of water and food.

On April 24, Shackleton and his five companions climbed into *James Caird* and set off for South Georgia. The twenty-two men left on Elephant Island stood on the cold, rocky beach, watching until the tiny boat disappeared over the horizon.

With the wind filling *James Caird*'s small sail, Worsley guided the little boat through the pack. By nightfall, they had reached the open waters of the South Atlantic Ocean. It was a seething nightmare of huge swells and towering waves.

On the morning of April 24, James Caird is launched from the rocky beach of Elephant Island.

By dawn the next day, they had sailed forty-five miles from Elephant Island. Shackleton organized the men into two watches. While he, Crean, and McNeish steered the boat, tended the sail, and bailed out the frigid water that continually washed over the sides, Worsley, McCarthy, and Vincent tried to sleep in the soggy, cramped space below the canvas cover. Every four hours, the men of each watch traded places.

On the third day, the sun peeked between the clouds long enough for Worsley to take a reading of their position. By his calculations, they had sailed 128 miles from Elephant Island. In the afternoon, the wind increased to gale force, whipping the sea's surface into enormous waves. For two days, the wind screamed incessantly. All the men could do was steer and bail and pray that their little boat held together.

On the afternoon of the fifth day, the wind died and the skies cleared. Crashing waves gave way to huge swells that came at them one after another, like rolling mountains of water. First the boat would be swept up one side of a swell and then hurled at great speed down the other side. Then it was up the next, only to go swooping down again.

On the sixth day, the winds changed, pushing *James Caird* directly toward South Georgia. But the next day, the winds changed again, coming up directly from the south. Bitterly cold, the wind lashed at the boat and pushed up waves that crashed over the side. Fearing they might capsize, Shackleton had the men take down the sail. To keep the boat from spinning around in the water, they made a sea anchor out of a canvas bag tied to a rope. As the bag dragged in the water, it kept the boat headed into the wind.

The wind was so cold that the spray from the waves froze instantly when it splashed onto the boat. For a while, no one noticed the ice forming. But as *James Caird* began to ride lower in the water, they realized the boat was covered with a layer of ice that was getting thicker—and heavier—by the minute. If they didn't remove it, they would sink. All through the night, in total darkness, the men chipped away ice from the hull, the mast, the ropes—every part of the boat they could reach. Shackleton kept a close eye on his companions. If he noticed a man reaching the point of exhaustion, he ordered a hot drink made for everyone.

The skies cleared on the tenth day. With a bright sun beaming down on them, Worsley rechecked their position.

They had covered 444 miles since leaving Elephant Island. They were more than halfway to South Georgia!

For several more days, the clear weather held. Mile by mile, they drew closer to their destination. On May 7, they spotted clumps of seaweed in the water and seabirds overhead. Land was near!

At half past noon on May 8, their fifteenth day at sea, McCarthy let out a great shout: "Land!" The others squinted at the spot on the horizon where he pointed. Yes, it was land—they could just make out jagged mountain peaks covered with snow. Worsley's navigating had been perfect. South Georgia lay dead ahead.

In this painting, JAMES CAIRD approaches South Georgia Island after fifteen days crossing the world's stormiest ocean.

As *James Caird* drew closer to shore, the wind increased, whipping the sea into mountains of foam and spray. Shackleton knew if they tried to land under such conditions, the waves would hurl them against the rocks. For hours, they fought against the wind and waves, trying to maintain their position in the water. As darkness fell, their strength was almost gone. Then, quite suddenly, the wind changed direction, making it possible for them to land.

In the pale light of dawn, Shackleton assessed their situation. He spotted a small beach near the back of a bay. But shielding the bay was a line of half-submerged boulders. Shackleton watched and waited. When he barked out the order, *James Caird* sailed quickly toward a narrow opening among the boulders. At the last minute, they had to veer sharply away to avoid being dashed against the rocks. Again and again they tried and failed. Finally, on the fifth attempt, *James Caird* slipped safely through the line of boulders and into the bay. Then the boat's bow ran aground on the beach. They had made it.

For seventeen days, they had battled the sea, the wind, and the cold. Against all odds, they were safely on South Georgia. But the whaling stations all lay on the other side of the island. They had to keep moving.

The gaps between the rocks offered four different routes into the island's interior. But which gap should they choose?

8

CROSSING SOUTH GEORGIA

Shackleton was anxious to get to a whaling station. Every day of delay in rescuing the men on Elephant Island might mean the death of one or more of them. But he and his five companions were exhausted. McCarthy, McNeish, and Vincent were in such bad condition that they could hardly walk. For several days, Shackleton let the men rest and recover. Then he told them what he had decided to do next.

Since the whaling stations lay on the other side of South Georgia from where *James Caird* had landed, they could try to reach them by sailing around the island. But *James Caird* was so battered that Shackleton didn't think

Rugged and forbidding, the interior of South Georgia Island is a maze of steep mountains and crevasse-filled glaciers.

it would survive another journey. The only other option, as he saw it, was to travel overland, across the mountains. Shackleton guessed the distance to be about twenty-two miles.

Always the optimist, Shackleton gave the others the impression that he had no doubt that crossing South Georgia was possible. Yet he knew no one had ever done it before. There were no maps of the island's interior. Crossing it meant traveling through completely unknown territory.

Shackleton chose Worsley and Crean to accompany him on this overland journey. Vincent and McCarthy were still too weak for mountain climbing. He left McNeish in charge of looking after them.

Early on the morning of May 19, 1916, Shackleton, Worsley, and Crean set out for Stromness, the closest whaling station on the island's opposite coast. Because he wanted to travel as fast as possible, Shackleton chose not to take along tents or sleeping bags. They carried a three-day supply of food, a small stove, two compasses, binoculars, a coil of rope, and a small ax.

It took several hours to climb up the steep snow-covered slope behind the beach. The view from the top was spectacular—and terrifying. Before them was a jumble of jagged mountain peaks, glaciers, and snowfields. But Shackleton knew that no matter how difficult and dangerous the journey, they had to get across the island.

Shackleton, Crean, and Worsley headed toward what they thought was a frozen lake. But the lake turned out to be a bay, a finger of ocean water jutting deeply inland. Since the cliffs were too steep to climb, they had to retrace many of their steps and then head in a different direction. They traveled all night, not stopping until the next morning to eat a quick meal.

Less than an hour later, they were on the move again, marching toward a peak where five huge outcroppings of rock stood like the fingers on a giant hand. The gaps between the rocks offered four different routes into the island's interior. But which gap should they choose? Shackleton chose the closest one. But when they reached it, they found a sheer cliff on the other side that plunged to a glacier far below. There was no way they could get down. Frustrated, they retraced their steps. Then they tried the second gap. It, too, turned out to be impassable, as did the third. Desperately, they struggled to the top of the fourth gap.

The view from the fourth pass was more encouraging. Directly below them there was a short, steep cliff. But below that lay a long slope of snow that led down into the island's interior. They couldn't tell what lay at the bottom of the slope—it was hidden by thick fog.

Shackleton stood thoughtfully for a moment. The sun had set, and it would soon be dark. The temperature was dropping quickly. If they stayed where they were and waited for morning, they would freeze to death without sleeping bags and a tent. They had to risk going down into whatever lay below.

Thirty minutes later, they reached the bottom of the cliff. Poised at the top of the snow slope, Shackleton turned to his companions. Instead of climbing down, he asked, what if they slid? Coiling the rope on the snow to form a sort of sled, they sat down with Shackleton in the front, Crean in the back, and Worsley sandwiched in between. Holding tightly to each other, they pushed off and went whooshing down the slope into the darkness below.

Miraculously, they didn't fall into a crevasse or smash into rocks. The slope simply leveled out, and they slid gently to a stop. Laughing with relief, they dusted themselves off and shook each other's hands.

The fog lifted, and by the light of the moon they pressed on, sometimes walking, sometimes climbing, but always as fast as they could. After many hours, they realized with growing excitement that some of the peaks and valleys around them looked familiar. *Endurance* had sailed past this part of the island when it had arrived at South Georgia in 1914. They were close! As the sun rose on their third day of climbing, they reached the top of a ridge and looked down on a bay they recognized instantly as Fortuna Bay. Beyond the next ridge of mountains, they knew, were Stromness Bay and a whaling station.

With their goal so close, Shackleton decided they had the time to rest for a moment and eat a hot meal. While the last of their food cooked in the pot, he climbed a ridge for a better view. Above the sighing of the wind, he thought he heard a whistle blow. A little later, all three men heard the sound again. It was the morning whistle of a whaling station! Shackleton knew the whistle meant there were people at the station. And if there were people, there would be ships.

Shackleton's destination: a whaling station in Stromness Bay

Full of hope, Shackleton, Crean, and Worsley clambered down the icy cliffs on one side of Fortuna Bay and up those on the other side. A few hours later, they stood on the last ridge, looking down at Stromness Bay and the whaling station. They could see people moving between the buildings. Two ships were anchored in the bay. With tears in their eyes, they shook each other's hands. They had done it!

At three o'clock in the afternoon on May 20, 1916, the three men staggered into the station. Two children saw them. Frightened by the men's filthy, torn clothes and long scraggly beards and hair, they ran away.

Shackleton walked up to a man and asked that he take them to the station manager. The man led them to the manager's house. They knocked and the manager came to the door. The manager stared at the three men and asked gruffly, "Well?"

"My name is Shackleton," the Boss replied.

The manager was stunned. Like everyone else who knew of the *Endurance* expedition, he thought the Boss and his men had died long ago. Seeing Shackleton was like seeing a ghost.

Shackleton, Worsley, and Crean basked in the warm hospitality of the whaling station. They took baths, shaved, and cut their shaggy hair. They dressed in clean clothes. And they ate. After a diet of little more than seal meat for many months, they feasted on foods their bodies craved—fresh bread, fruit, cakes, and cookies. Clean, warm, and finally well fed, Shackleton could only think of the twenty-two men still marooned on Elephant Island.

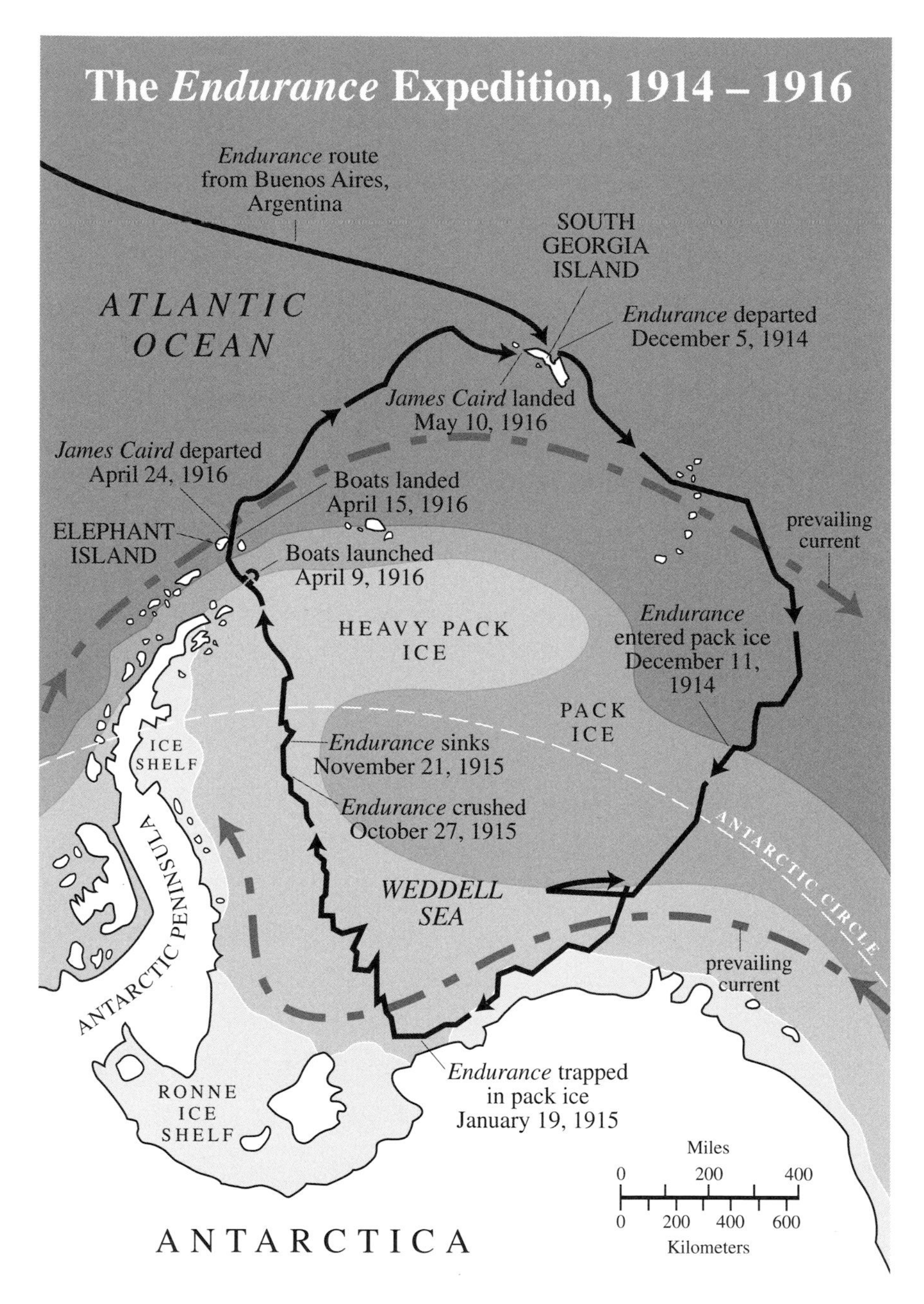

This maps shows the path taken by Shackleton's ENDURANCE *expedition. Currents in the Weddell Sea moved the pack ice—and the men stranded on it—northward along the Antarctic Peninsula.*

Winter had already begun. The whalers offered to help in any way they could.

The station manager immediately arranged for a whaling ship to sail around the island and pick up McNeish, McCarthy, and Vincent. Then he and Shackleton sat down to plan the rescue of the men on Elephant Island.

On May 23, just three days after reaching Stromness Bay, Shackleton, Worsley, and Crean were aboard a Norwegian steamship, *Southern Sky,* that had been anchored in the bay. They headed toward Elephant Island at top speed.

But Antarctica was already well into the polar winter. The countless floes that made up the pack had begun to freeze into a solid layer on the sea surface. Sixty miles from Elephant Island, *Southern Sky* was stopped by the ice. It was not strong enough to break through. Shackleton was frustrated beyond words. He was so close to his stranded men, yet unable to reach them. He asked the captain of *Southern Sky* to steam to the Falkland Islands, just off the tip of South America. Perhaps there, Shackleton thought, he could find a ship strong enough to batter its way through the pack to Elephant Island.

From the Falklands, Shackleton sent a telegram to England, explaining what had happened to the expedition and his need for a ship to reach Elephant Island. When Emily heard the news, she said little in public. But she was immensely relieved to learn that Ernest was alive.

In the Falklands, however, Shackleton discovered there were no ships to be had for a rescue operation. Desperate, he turned to the governments of Uruguay, Argentina, and Chile for help. Uruguay responded the most quickly.

Officials offered him a small but strong ship, *Pesca,* and its crew. On June 17, *Pesca* headed southward. Three days later, Shackleton, Crean, and Worsley spotted the snow-capped peaks of Elephant Island on the horizon. But just twenty miles from the island, thick pack ice barred the way—too thick for *Pesca* to ram its way through.

Twice the pack had defeated Shackleton's attempts to reach his stranded men. Almost sick with worry for their safety, Shackleton asked *Pesca's* captain to sail to Punta Arenas, Chile. There, Shackleton chartered another ship, *Emma.* In mid-July, it came within one hundred miles of Elephant Island. But like *Pesca, Emma* was unable to break through the pack and was forced to turn back.

Once more, Shackleton turned to Chile for help. This time, he was given *Yelcho,* a small steel-hulled steamship. On August 25, Shackleton, Crean, and Worsley headed southward yet again.

On August 30, 1916, Marston, the artist on *Endurance,* was looking out to sea, making sketches. It had been 137 days since *James Caird* had left for South Georgia. As Marston scanned the horizon, he spotted what looked like a ship far in the distance. It *was* a ship! Within minutes, all the men lined the beach, shouting, screaming, and waving.

On board *Yelcho,* Shackleton grabbed a pair of binoculars and trained them on the beach. He began to count the men standing there. When he reached twenty-two, it seemed as if the weight of the world was suddenly lifted off his shoulders. All his men were alive!

A small boat was lowered over *Yelcho's* side. The Boss climbed aboard and stood in the bow as it was rowed to shore. He spotted Frank Wild and called out to him, asking if all of the men were well. "We are all well, Boss!" Wild answered. An hour later, Shackleton's men were safely aboard *Yelcho*. The little ship turned, leaving Elephant Island in the distance.

On September 3, 1916, *Yelcho* steamed into Punta Arenas. A huge crowd waited at the docks to welcome the lost explorers back to civilization. Ernest sent a quick letter to Emily. In it, he summed up the ordeal: "I have done it . . . not a life lost and we have been through Hell."

Rescued at last! The lifeboat from YELCHO (BACKGROUND) lands on Elephant Island to pick up Shackleton's stranded men.

The strain of all that had transpired on the ENDURANCE expedition had taken its toll. At first Shackleton thought of going to the Arctic, but the pull of Antarctica was too strong.

9

QUEST

The men of *Endurance* returned to a world that was caught up in the horror of World War I. When the expedition members arrived back in England, most joined the war effort. Several were killed in action.

Shackleton, however, did not return with his men. He headed for Ross Island to pick up the relief party that had survived terrible conditions to lay down the food stoves that Shackleton's southern party never picked up. It wasn't until May 1917 that Ernest Shackleton was finally back in England and reunited with Emily and their three children.

With so many of his men involved in the war effort, he wanted to participate as well. But at age forty-two, Shackleton was too old to fight. Later that year, however, the British war office sent him to South America.

Emily and her son Edward stroll through a London park, shortly after learning that Ernest and the men of the ENDURANCE were safe.

After six months, Shackleton completed his work in South America. He returned to England but was soon traveling again when the government sent him to northern Russia as a polar expert to help with British military activities. Frank Wild and Frank Worsley were assigned to the same post, along with several other members of the *Endurance* crew.

When the war ended, Shackleton turned his attention to writing a book about the *Endurance* expedition. Called *South,* it was published in 1919 and sold well. With money earned from book sales, lectures, and Hurley's photographs and movies of the expedition, Shackleton was finally able to pay off most of his debts.

But there was little left over with which to support himself and his family. It was a discouraging time.

It wasn't long before Shackleton began to dream of another journey to polar regions, even though he was not in very good health. The strain of all that had transpired on the *Endurance* expedition had taken its toll. At first Shackleton thought of going to the Arctic, but the pull of Antarctica was too strong. He proposed a new expedition, with the goal of sailing all the way around the Antarctic continent and possibly mapping parts of the interior. After he had gotten the financial backing he needed, Shackleton felt he had purpose in his life again. His old energy and enthusiasm returned.

Shackleton wrote to some of the men who had been on *Endurance* and invited them to come along on his new expedition. Both Wild and Worsley jumped at the chance. So did Dr. Alexander Macklin, who had been the doctor on *Endurance.* Over the years, he and Shackleton had become very good friends.

Shackleton bought a Norwegian vessel that Emily suggested he name *Quest.* Loaded with supplies, *Quest* set out from England on September 17, 1921, and crossed the Atlantic to South America.

In Rio de Janeiro, Shackleton became very ill. But he refused to let anyone examine him, even Dr. Macklin. He also refused to let *Quest* return to England. Shackleton rested, appeared to recover, and the expedition continued. *Quest* set sail for South Georgia and arrived there on January 4, 1922. As *Quest* followed the rugged coastline, Shackleton and Worsley stood together on the deck, ex-

Shackleton waves to well-wishers as QUEST sets sail from England in 1921.

citedly pointing out to each other familiar landmarks from their journey across the island's interior six years earlier. Shackleton was delighted to be back.

That afternoon, Shackleton and his men went ashore at the Grytviken whaling station. They renewed old friendships and walked up into the steep hills above the station to get a view of *Quest* from a distance. That night, during dinner aboard the ship, Shackleton was in high spirits. He went to bed, talking about how good it would be to see Antarctica again.

But in the early hours of January 5, Macklin heard a noise in Shackleton's cabin and went in to check on him. He found the Boss lying, shivering, under a single thin blanket.

Tucking another blanket around his friend, Macklin told Shackleton he should take better care of himself and not work so hard. To this Shackleton replied, "You are always wanting me to give up things, what is it I ought to give up?"

Seconds later, Shackleton suffered a massive heart attack and died. He was forty-seven years old.

At dawn the next day, Frank Wild assembled the men on deck and broke the bad news: the Boss was dead. Wild asked Leonard Hussey, who had also been on *Endurance,* to accompany Shackleton's body to South America and, from there, to England. As for the expedition, Wild assumed command, and *Quest* sailed southward, as he was certain Shackleton would have wished.

When Hussey arrived in South America, he sent a telegram with the news of Ernest's death to Emily. Emily sent a quick reply. Bury him on South Georgia, she wrote.

Members of the QUEST expedition erected this cross on South Georgia's coast as a memorial to Ernest Shackleton.

It seemed to her the most fitting place for his final resting place, close to the frozen continent he had been drawn to all his life. Hussey took Shackleton's body back to South Georgia Island. On March 5, 1922, Sir Ernest Shackleton was buried in a small graveyard near Grytviken, among the graves of Norwegian whalers, not far from the edge of the sea where icebergs drifted slowly past.

When Frank Wild brought *Quest* back to South Georgia on May 3, 1922, the men aboard climbed a steep hill overlooking Grytviken. At the top, they buried a signed photograph of the expedition members beneath a pile of stones topped with a cross, in memory of the Boss.

KEEPING WARM IN THE WORLD'S COLDEST PLACE

The interior of Antarctica is the coldest place on the earth. The lowest temperature recorded on the continent was –129.3° Fahrenheit (F). That measurement was taken in the winter of 1983 at a Russian research station located several hundred miles from the South Pole.

For Ernest Shackleton, Robert Falcon Scott, and other Antarctic explorers, cold was a serious threat to survival. Sledging parties, moving slowly southward toward the Pole in the Antarctic spring and summer, routinely encountered temperatures of –20° to –30° F on the Great Ice Barrier. As they climbed the glaciers cutting through the Transantarctic Mountains, temperatures dropped to –60° to –75° F.

Then there was the wind. During Antarctic blizzards, winds may blow with hurricane force, near 120 miles per hour. When high winds and intense cold combine, exposed skin can freeze very quickly. Frostbite, where skin and underlying tissue freezes solid, was something Shackleton and his men often faced. Fingers, toes, and noses are most at risk from frostbite. If not warmed quickly and carefully, frostbitten tissue dies and can develop into a life-threatening infection called gangrene. One *Endurance* crewmember's toes were so badly frostbitten during the seven days spent in the lifeboats that they developed gangrene. The ship's doctors had to amputate some of his toes when the men reached Elephant Island.

To survive the Antarctic cold, a person needs warm, dry, windproof clothing and a good diet that is high in calories. The early explorers' clothes were mostly made of wool—even their underwear! A hooded jacket and pants, both cotton, formed the outermost layer. The cotton fabric was very tightly woven, though, making it nearly windproof. The explorers' warmest mittens and boots were reindeer hide, with the furry side facing out. Reindeer hide was warmer than leather and didn't crack in extreme cold. But even so, Shackleton and his men often had a hard time keeping their feet and hands from becoming frostbitten.

It was in their diet that many of the early Antarctic explorers fell short. Manhauling heavy sledges across rough ice and through deep snow is terribly hard work and burns many calories. On top of that, explorers needed extra calories simply to stay warm. They could easily burn 5,000 calories or more a day manhauling in the cold. Scott and, later, Shackleton seriously underestimated the amount of food needed on a journey to the Pole. Even when members of the southern parties were eating full sledging rations, they were probably getting only 4,000 to 4,200 calories a day. And as food supplies dwindled and rations were cut, they had to get by on less than half that amount. It's hard to imagine how hungry, exhausted, and cold the men were as they trekked to the Pole.

How did they do it? Fierce determination and courage were important factors. And for the men serving under Ernest Shackleton, the Boss' unfailing optimism was key to their safely surviving every ordeal.

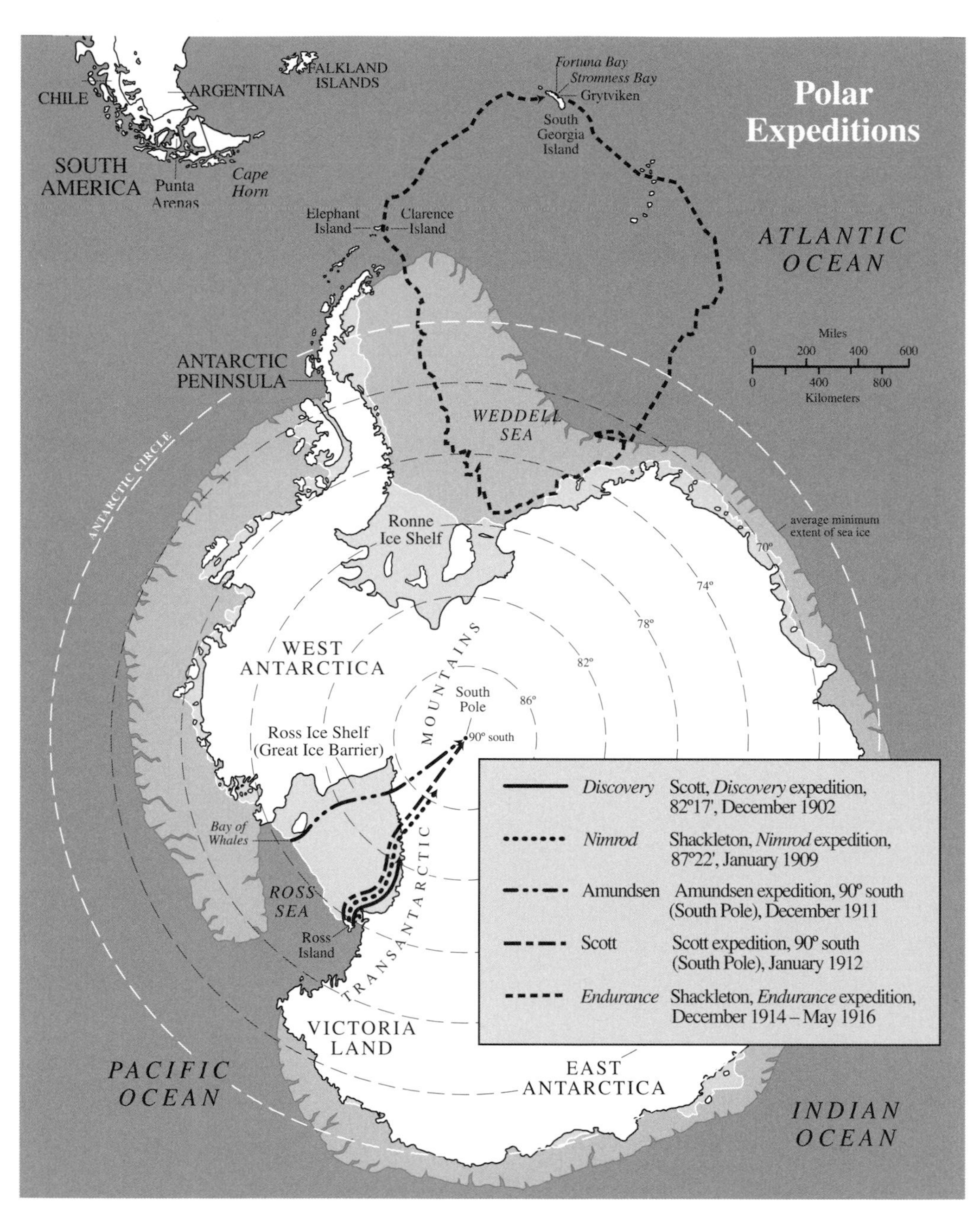

Shackleton tried unsuccessfully to reach the South Pole, with Scott in 1902 and on his own in 1908. His ENDURANCE expedition failed to reach land but became one of the greatest polar adventures of all time.

Source Notes

p. 11 Kim Heacox, *Shackleton: The Antarctic Challenge* (Washington, D.C.: National Geographic Society, 1999), 39.

p. 19 James Dunmore, *The United Methodist* (4 May 1922): 213.

p. 31 Sir Ernest Shackleton diary, 8 February 1902, Scott Polar Research Institute, Cambridge.

p. 37 Roland Huntford, *Shackleton* (New York: Atheneum, 1986), 110.

p. 42 Ibid., 140.

p. 52 Shackleton diary, 9 January 1909. (Huntford, p. 273)

p. 60 Caroline Alexander, *The Endurance: Shackleton's Legendary Antarctic Expedition* (New York: Alfred E. Knopf, 1998), 9.

p. 61 Heacox, *Shackleton,* 56.

p. 66 Frank Arthur Worsley, *Endurance: An Epic of Polar Adventure* (New York: W. W. Norton & Company, 1931), 4.

p. 72 Alexander, *The Endurance,*109.

p. 79 Ibid., 123.

p. 86 T. H. Baughman, *Shackleton of the Antarctic* (Tallahassee, Florida: Eöthen Press, 2002), 71.

p. 93 Sir Ernest Shackleton, *South,* ed. Peter King (London: Century, 1991), 149.

p. 97 Ibid., 155.

p. 97 Sir Ernest Shackleton to Emily Shackleton, 3 September 1916, Scott Polar Research Institute, Cambridge.

p. 102 A. H. Macklin diary, 5 January 1922, Macklin family papers, Aberdeen.

Bibliography

Alexander, Caroline. *The Endurance: Shackleton's Legendary Antarctic Expedition.* New York: Alfred E. Knopf, 1998.

Armstrong, Jennifer. *Shipwreck at the Bottom of the World.* New York: Crown Publishers, 1998.

Baughman, T. H. *Shackleton of the Antarctic.* Tallahassee, FL: Eöthen Press, 2002.

Heacox, Kim. *Shackleton: The Antarctic Challenge.* Washington, D.C.: National Geographic Society, 1999.

Huntford, Roland. *Shackleton.* New York: Atheneum, 1985.

Kimmel, Elizabeth Cody. *Ice Story: Shackleton's Lost Expedition.* New York: Clarion Books, 1999.

Lansing, Alfred. *Endurance: Shackleton's Incredible Voyage.* New York: Carroll & Graf Publishers, 1986.

Mill, Hugh Robert. *The Life of Sir Ernest Shackleton.* Boston: Little, Brown & Company, 1923.

Shackleton, Sir Ernest. *The Heart of the Antarctic.* Philadelphia: J. B. Lippincott Company, 1909.

———. *South.* New York: Heinemann, 1919.

———. *South: The Story of Shackleton's Last Expedition, 1914–1917.* Edited by Peter King. London: Century, 1991.

Worsley, Frank Arthur. *Endurance: An Epic of Polar Adventure.* New York: W. W. Norton & Company, 1931.

———. *Shackleton's Boat Journey.* New York: W.W. Norton, 1977.

Other Resources

The Endurance: Shackleton's Legendary Antarctic Expedition. (documentary). George Butler, dir. White Mountains Films, 2000.

Lynn Rosentrater and Planet Interactive for the Museum of Science, Boston. "Secrets of the Ice: An Antarctic Expedition." *Secrets of the Ice from the Museum of Science, Boston.* <http://www.secretsoftheice.org/> 2002.

PBS. "Shackleton's Voyage of the *Endurance*," *Nova Online.* <http://www.pbs.org/wgbh/nova/shackleton> 2002.

Royal Geographic Society. *Welcome to the Royal Geographic Society.* <http://www.rgs.org/> 2002.

Scott Polar Research Institute, University of Cambridge. *Scott Polar Research Institute.* <http://www.spri.cam.ac.uk/> 2002.

Shackleton's Antarctic Adventure (giant-screen film). WGBH and White Mountains Films, 2001.

Shackleton (made-for-television film and video). Charles Sturridge, dir. A&E Network Studios, 2002.

INDEX

The photographs and illustrations in this book are used with the permission of: Library of Congress, (background) pp. 2–3, 6–7, 14, 25, 40, 55, 69, 77, 88, 98, 104–105; © Royal Geographical Society, pp. 2 (foreground), 6 (foreground), 27, 32, 34, 38, 45, 49, 52, 54, 59, 62, 64, 65, 67, 68, 70, 72, 73, 84, 86, 92, 97; © Scott Polar Research Institute, University of Cambridge, pp. 11, 13; © Bettmann/CORBIS, pp. 15, 41; Hulton|Archive by Getty Images, pp. 21, 56, 58, 81, 101, 102; Laura Westlund, pp. 22–23, 94, 106; © Hulton-Deutsch Collection/CORBIS, pp. 29; © Academy of Natural Sciences of Philadelphia/CORBIS, p. 46; National Oceanic and Atmospheric Administration Photo Library, p. 89; the British Library, p. 99.

Cover: © Royal Geographic Society [Sir E. Shackleton and Football on the Ice]
Back cover: courtesy of the Library of Congress.